NOW AND

Art Now at Tate Britain

First published 2004 by order of the Tate Trustees
by Tate Britain
in association with
Tate Publishing, a division of Tate Enterprises Ltd,
Millbank, London SW1P 4RG
www.tate.org.uk/publishing

To document Art Now at Tate Britain

British Library Cataloguing in Publication Data
A catalogue record for this book is available from the British Library

ISBN 1-85437-600-4

Distributed in the United States and Canada by Harry N. Abrams, Inc., New York

Library of Congress Cataloging in Publication Data
Library of Congress Control Number: 2004112678

Designed by Marit Münzberg
Printed in Belgium by Snoeck-Ducaju & Zoon

Front cover
Roger Hiorns, *Vauxhall* 2003 (detail), Courtesy the artist and Corvi-Mora, London

Foreword

Art Now at Tate Britain is a platform for new work and emerging practice in contemporary British art. Today's artists make memorable and important shows in an ever-widening range of situations, but the Art Now series offers a particular challenge: to present new work in a major public museum, often for the first time in an artist's career. This book documents and reflects upon the series of projects presented between Spring 2003 and Autumn 2004, and offers a number of intriguing glimpses of current and future directions.

Tate Britain's engagement with contemporary art takes many forms: contemporary acquisition displays, the Turner Prize, the Duveens commission, the Tate Triennial exhibition, as well as major monographic surveys. But it is important to the life of the museum and its visitors that we offer an ongoing platform for young artists throughout the year. For that reason we have increased the number of Art Now projects from three to five a year, and initiated the Art Now Lightbox programme – occasional presentations of exemplary single-channel film and video works, held in a new projection space.

We owe huge thanks to the artists who responded to our invitation with such enthusiasm and purpose. Individually and collectively, they have brought a palpable energy to the Art Now programme. The artists were selected by Lizzie Carey-Thomas, Mary Horlock and Katharine Stout, curators at Tate Britain, following studio visits across the country and conversations with many colleagues at Tate and beyond. In this publication they explore the strong connections that emerge between the discrete projects they curated. Their drive and vision have resulted in a compelling series, as Martin Herbert's thoughtful essay testifies.

Art Now relies on the professionalism and enthusiasm of a great many individuals. Thanks are due to Tamsin Dillon, Platform for Art, London Underground, for our collaboration on the Muntean /Rosenblum project, and to Stephen Bode, Film & Video Umbrella, for help and advice. At Tate, I would like to thank Gregor Muir, Kramlich Curator of Contemporary Art, who advised on the first Lightbox programme. Many other colleagues contributed to the success of the series including Ray Burns, Olivia Colling, Simeon Corless, Claire Eva, Bronwyn Gardner, Kenneth Graham, Mikei Hall, Sarah Hyde, Anna Nesbit, Gemma Nightingale, Heidi Reitmaier, Andy Shiel and Tate Photography. Thanks also to Marit Münzberg for her design work on this publication, and the leaflets accompanying this series.

We are delighted to have Diesel as sponsor of the Art Now programme, supporting Tate Britain's commitment to new departures in contemporary art.

Judith Nesbitt
Head of Exhibitions and Displays, Tate Britain

Art Now

We are gliding down the Danube. A ruggedly handsome middle-aged man, neatly dressed and backed by a seven-piece band, is singing a melancholy song entitled *Who Doesn't Know How to Suffer, Doesn't Know How to Love* to a woman, the Yugoslavia-born, UK-based artist Breda Beban. Presently, as the blue river's route takes our raft past the grim Stalinist architecture of Belgrade on one side and a mysterious forest on the other, the minstrel music will move into a higher, more defiantly celebratory gear, and Beban will perform a dance. It is a traditional Balkan dance, one that involves the dancer stepping forwards over three chairs: the one she has just left is taken from behind and placed in front of her so that she can continually move on, stepping into air and hoping others will provide some solidity for her. The work of an artist forced to leave her homeland when it was torn asunder by war, it is inevitably read as a dance of exile. And it gives her video work, *Walk of Three Chairs* 2003, its title.

This bittersweet compound of geographic and societal fragmentation, loss and trust, grimly symbolic face-offs between concrete and clover, and ancient traditions gracefully persisting under tectonic pressure – this is art, now. Or it's art now as defined by the first entry in Tate Britain's Art Now Lightbox series, the newest and most flexible aspect of its Art Now programme, shown in the week of 23–30 May 2003. A week later Beban's DVD would be replaced by the work of another artist, then another, in a series that continued for two months (and was later followed by a second and then third set of videos). Apart from performances, surely no art exhibited in the history of Tate has had a faster turnaround than this. But perhaps we should not be surprised to see such new-found flexibility here. Tate Britain is not the same entity that opened the Art Now space in 1995. The name of the former has altered, that of the latter has stayed the same; neither, though, is precisely as once it was. The art has changed too, but then it would have to; the world has changed.

When Art Now was inaugurated, with an exhibition by the American artist Matthew Barney, it was something of a novelty. Dotted like grey daisies across Europe's capital and secondary cities are Kunsthallen – large, airy spaces that show contemporary art but are not commercial galleries – and this small space tucked away at the end of the Duveen Galleries in the Tate (as was) suggested a kind of micro-Kunsthalle within a museum. However, the artists initially featured were often quite well-established and the programme moved at the pace of that museum – that is to say, stately, like the rotating space station in the film *2001*.

But although curatorial portholes on the wider movements of contemporary art were rare in visual arts museums at the time, they are less so now (when millionaires who launch private museums for their collections reserve rooms for comparatively untried practitioners, when corporations convert their lobbies into venues for ticklish slices of institutional critique). In part, this is a function of a broader cultural shift in which the idea of contemporariness – of 'being up to speed', in the oxygenated argot of business – is a prime currency. All over the world, monolithic art institutions are being systematically softened, self-punctured and made user-friendly. This is not to say that the aim is always cynical, or that such a process isn't worthwhile simply because it's voguish – Art Now being a prescient case in point – but to recognise that there are historical forces at work; that Art Now doesn't exist in a vacuum.

But that's not the whole story. The proliferation of such liminal spaces in museums is also a pragmatic reflection of the increased velocity with which artists now pass through the system and into their halls. Artists are being given major-space career retrospectives before the age of thirty-five. Their work is bought by museums when they are even younger, and these institutions are increasingly staffed by a young generation of curators and buyers. And in many major cities, but particularly over the past decade in London, there have sprung up so many commercial and, though less so lately, so-called alternative art spaces as to create the illusion – which may not be an illusion – that there is more contemporary art being made, that this continues to be a rich moment of cultural production. In such a combustible climate, where today's East End group-show denizen is tomorrow's surprise hit at an edgy biennale and the day after's fashion magazine-approved aesthetic force, institutions that ignore developments in contemporary art risk coming across as ostriches. Those that take the time and energy to be responsive, however, can do something more than the equivalent of pouring champagne over someone who's already crossed the finishing line; they can spur on a runner mid-race, and at the decibel-level that only major institutional lungpower can muster.

For viewers and, I've been given to understand, for artists too, an exhibition in Art Now is a uniquely hybrid experience, and not only because the space feels architecturally different from the rest of the building. For anyone who, like me and like the generation of artists currently being shown there, grew up BTM – Before Tate Modern – the honour is an almost nostalgic one: to receive *an exhibition in the Tate*, the immovable culture palace where so many young British dreamers have received their first taste of advanced art. It carries over all of that residual gravity. In recent years Tate Britain has changed, mostly for the better, as various layers of accreted fustian have been shaken off. As an artist who fairly recently had a solo show at Tate Britain said to me, the place feels like a zone of possibility on the basis that its identity still holds itself up usefully for ongoing redefinition: of contemporary British art, and of all those terms taken individually. I say all this only in order to assay the fluctuating weight of history. And regardless of how art is nuanced by the building and its history, I have seen the potential level of exposure engender an excitable quaking in certain younger artists invited to participate in Art Now – which brings us to its other blindingly advantageous aspect, the sheer force of numbers passing through Tate Britain's turnstiles on a daily basis. For artists this is a calibre of exposure that simply can't be obtained in most venues.

And yet, and yet … this is not simply another room in Tate Britain's stone labyrinth. The Art Now space feels – and increasingly so recently – like a world apart: in the institution but not quite *of* it. It's as if all the historical credibility (and pressure) attached to Tate Britain hangs around at the Art Now door; or as if it were a mantle being dropped off at the cloakroom, left there to be draped over one's shoulders on exiting. The space itself seems a strange ingress, a proving ground within that aforementioned zone of possibility. On most days it's the nerviest corner of the building. While Tate Britain has speeded up its responsiveness of late, giving monographic shows to photographers, allowing some quite unlikely sculptural events to take place in the Duveens, and mounting a triennial of contemporary British art, Art Now appears to be the wellspring of these changes, and it's here that the water moves at a faster pace. In the past season, under the joint curatorship of Lizzie Carey-Thomas, Mary Horlock and Katharine Stout, the programme has become increasingly reactive and accelerated. It has focused on younger artists – either British or UK-based, or working in the UK, as is Tate Britain's remit – with shorter, more frequent and more dynamic exhibitions, and, of course, the addition of the Lightbox series, which recognises and accommodates the increasing primacy of film and video art.

I'll say it again: the art has changed, and you can see this clearly in the latest sequence of Art Now exhibitions. Blame it on biennales, the Internet, or whatever you like, but our East End group-show denizen is as likely to have issues in common with artists working in Seoul or Johannesburg or Mexico City as with the person working next door to them in Acme Studios; and issues that permeate the Esperanto of contemporary art pervade these shows. To explain how, one could draw a diagram full of circled concepts and arrows firing off from them. In lieu of that, here's one big concept I'd circle: a sense of loss, of something having gone. And this is not a theoretical sense – like that laid on the ivory fish-slab of postmodernism – but an emotional response, like something one might experience when coming out of shock.

What's gone? A lot. In Roger Hiorns' *Vauxhall* 2003, where flames snake out of a grate, outside the museum, it's the idea of holy fire and of longed-for religious verity; what's left is an ongoing flaring up of something that's simply a chemical reaction. In Mark Titchner's work, *Be Angry But Don't Stop Breathing* 2003, it's the divisional space around previously revolutionary philosophies of mind, now melded into a new-age smorgasbord for the terminally confused in which pop lyrics might have as much validity as the Orgone theories of Wilheim Reich. In Ian Kiaer's sallow, lyrical sculptures and in the silent, frictionless Steadicam ride of Mark Lewis's video of south London's Heygate Estate (*Children's Games* 2002) it's the hopeful idea of architecture embodying utopian concepts. In Saskia Olde Wolbers' video (*Placebo* 2002) it's the previously healthy life of the unseen hospitalised partici-pants, and, as editorialised by its narcotised imagery of dripping, softened objects, the boundary between reality and fantasy. In the sportswear-clad, philosophy-spouting zombies pictured by Muntean/Rosenblum it's the possibility of active, unbranded resistance to corporate desires, and the notion of an authentic and lasting counterculture. In Nigel Cooke's paintings it's nature as a hotline to the sublime. In Lucy McKenzie's installation which directs attention to the work of La Strada, it's women, conned and then illegally trafficked in Eastern Europe's sex trade. In Claire Barclay's carefully orchestrated installation it's our comforting familiarity with a known space and the hierarchical separation of art and craft. In Beban's film it's the possibility of ever going home again. And so on.

All of which is to drastically simplify and caricature what these particular artists do, to underplay the fact that many of them propose all kinds of consolatory aspects and new constellations of visual experience to fill their various vacuums. It pretends that artists' projects are not intrinsically resistant to easy literary capture and, heaven forbid, to clustering under thematic umbrellas. But it's worth suggest-ing that, despite the rush of cultural production, there appears to be a poignant haze of transition and dissolution and 'what now?' around the broader body of current contemporary art, and that this has been picked up by Art Now's radar. This is the case even when the work seems to look outward – as in David Musgrave's *trompe l'oeil* images of stick-figures, painted straight on the wall but resembling masking tape, or his sculptures that look like crumpled paper arranged loosely to resemble a figure but which are actually artfully creased pieces of painted steel. Musgrave is something of a connoisseur of conflicting textures and sensations, but there's always a ghostly echo of a body in his art, glimmering in and out of cognisance, and that idea of the body in limbo (he often refers in his titles to the figure of a golem, a mythical figure with a short, often violent life) is hard to shake from one's afterimage of his art.

Another thing to encircle is the encroaching presence of the real world. This is perhaps an issue of viewing, and of the impossibility of considering art as a separate, privileged space – in these interdisciplinary days art-making can come across as a visually oriented branch of anthropology or political science or avant-garde pop video-making. But it is an issue that cannot be extricated from the conditions of viewing now, not even in the case of, say, Katy Dove's sumptuous and otherworldy animations of coloured-pen doodles. Rising and falling in deep space or swooping over her father's old watercolour landscapes, they similarly play dandyish games with figuration and abstraction and, in the process, conjure up an uncertainty in the viewer about how seriously to take them. This, it seems, is art that wants to be provisional; that wants to travel light and to please with references to sunnier days; that doesn't want to attempt grand statements in case some as-yet-unseen hammer comes down and smashes them. Dove's work (shown, notably, in the Lightbox series when the Glasgow-based artist had barely exhibited elsewhere in the capital) is light-years away from the Warhol-like tenor of Phil Collins's video *Baghdad Screentests* 2002, yet both are responses to the same chaotic and ever-shrinking planet: one documenting in sidelong fashion, one evading as if life depended on it.

Baghdad Screentests is soundtracked – or more specifically its placid, plaintive images are variously tilted, pumped-up and fully inverted in terms of what they *mean* – by British and American musicians including Elvis Presley ('I'll be as strong as a mountain …'), The Smiths ('Please, keep me in mind …'), Donna Summer ('Ooh, it's so good, it's so good, it's so good …'), Big Star ('Won't you let me walk you home from school?') as well as enthusiastic English covers of American songs and plenty of alt. country. They're love songs and often great ones, and this is a forcefully thought-provoking imposition. It's extraordinary how potent cheap music is; extraordinary, too, the extent to which pop and electronic music have permeated the art world in recent years. It seems likely that many artists have musician envy – the immediacy! the money! the fans! – as surely as musicians latently wish to be taken seriously as 'artists'. It also seems likely that artists realise there's little point in cordoning off these particular worlds when the same strictures no longer apply to any other territory. Art is rapacious. But it isn't often dumb, and if the throwaway quality of pop music modulates one's response to the art in its favour, or at least contrasts against its gravitas, then it has a place in the gallery.

We're talking about a widespread sense of evanescence and its analogues in reality. A decade ago, the British art world was permeated by a kind of quick-fix, eye-popping visual art – the actions of a patient still in shock, to extend my earlier rickety metaphor – which seemed to relish the short term in a world that, theorists said, had gone beyond the end of history. There has since then been no return to notions of longevity or stability but, rather, a bruised and less festive awareness of the short term. It's notable, in this regard, that the last Art Now season and, particularly, the Lightbox works have been permeated by music, whose very existence could be a metaphor for things not staying still or lasting: from the mixture of hesitant piano and out-and-out rock that soundtracks Ann Course and Paul Clark's bleak little animations, to the sonic collage of *Mixtape* 2002 by Oliver Payne and Nick Relph, to Breda Beban's revenant wailing, to the melancholy piano playing that helps elevate Lucy McKenzie's collaborative video with Paulina Olowska (*Oblique Composition* 2003) into a realm of weird but sincere Modernist pastiche. Music is in the air and then gone, leaving a memory. It's a moment passed through, like the days to be ticked off with good deeds done on McKenzie's wall chart (*MMIV* 2003), a temporarily brightened state of affairs, like the bolt of opalescent lightning that hits the waste ground in one of Nigel Cooke's paintings.

This art is not throwaway, though it recognises that it might at any time be thrown. There is technique aplenty among these practices, from Cooke's virtuoso painting style to Musgrave's intricate and slow-burning deceptions to McKenzie's deft enquiry into the role of the artist. There are intelligent references to a golden past (Ian Kiaer's allusions to Brueghel; Muntean/Rosenblum's harking back to the hieratic poses of classical art; Cooke's invoking of the landscape tradition in general; Barclay's nods to the New Generation sculpture of 1960s Britain). There's ambition too, as always among young artists. But, crucially, there's no sense of a storing-up of putative new masterpieces against the ages. If one looks back on what has been included in Art Now during the past year, one finds little that had solidity, an air of permanence. Here, bodies transform and become virtualised and weightless; people are dragged across fragmented territories; ideologies become redundant and are reborn as pop culture; fire curls upwards, burns oxygen and is gone; lush scenery is streaked with graffiti; music graces the air and fades with a dying fall; a felt-tip fantasia reshapes itself on a momentary basis; a relationship turns out to have been one man's fantasy leading to a car crash. If there's a necessarily provisional quality about the Art Now programme as a whole, one that is implicit in its title – this is art now, and tomorrow, or in a few weeks, art will be something else – then it has found a sympathetic partner in the artworks that it has recently chosen to show: flares sent up from a world that, no longer sure if tomorrow will come or what it will look like, knows only that it will be different from today.

Martin Herbert

17 May – 6 July 2003   **Mark Titchner**

7 June – 31 August 2003   **Roger Hiorns**

19 July – 7 Sept 2003   **David Musgrave**

19 July – 14 Sept 2003   **Lightbox 1**
Breda Beban, Ann Course in collaboration
with Paul Clark, Mark Lewis,
Dan Holdsworth, Oliver Payne and Nick Relph,
Phil Collins, Jaki Irvine, Saskia Older Wolbers

20 Sept – 9 Nov 2003   **Lucy McKenzie**

22 Nov 2003 – 25 Jan 2004   **Ian Kiaer**

22 Nov – 15 Feb 2004   **Lightbox 2**
Daria Martin, Katy Dove, Haluk Acakçe,
Rob Kennedy & Stuart MacGregor

7 Feb – 28 March 2004   **Nigel Cooke**

17 April – 20 June 2004   **Muntean / Rosenblum**

3 July – 12 Sept 2004   **Claire Barclay**

3 July – 5 Sept 2004   **Lightbox 3**
Rosalind Nashashibi, Paul Morrison, John Wood & Paul Harrison

Mark Titchner

BE ANGRY BUT DON'T STOP BREATHING

Mark Titchner is fascinated by the myriad systems of belief that permeate contemporary culture. He often revisits defunct and outmoded philosophies, especially those born out of an avant-garde idealism which has long since waned. Conflicting theories are extracted from their historical framework and submitted to us for reappraisal, reassembled as hybrid installations incorporating wall paintings, vinyl banners, light boxes and hand-carved sculptures.

Whether combining song lyrics with the writings of the twentieth-century German philosopher Martin Heidegger or remaking 1960s scientific devices out of hardware store materials, Titchner's interest lies in the dissolution of boundaries, the migration of ideas and aesthetics from one discipline to another. His recent series of wall paintings constructed from airbrushed geometric shapes was initially based on his memories of the 1970s wallpaper he grew up with. He sees a trajectory originating from patterns in early abstract art, such as paintings by Kasimir Malevich or Joseph Albers, through to the homogenised patterns present in home décor, from high art to high street. A shared aesthetic persists without the conceptual or spiritual dimension that was fundamental to its origination. It is an examination of this cultural filtering process – the survival and popularisation of certain elements over and above others – which lies at the core of Titchner's practice.

In his installation BE ANGRY BUT DON'T STOP BREATHING, Titchner situates the gallery between the experimental forum of the laboratory and the devotional space of the cathedral. Through sculptural and text-based works, he conflates the philosophies of four cult figures whose theories were planted firmly outside scientific orthodoxy: Wilheim Reich MD, Marxist psychoanalyst and pioneer of Orgone energy; Arthur Janov, pioneer of Primal Therapy; Hans Jenny, natural scientist and inventor of Cymatics and Emmanuel Swedenborg, philosopher and theologian.

The central component of Titchner's installation is a laboriously hand-carved contraption, the latest in an ongoing series of semi-functional works that explore notions of ritual and devotion. Visitors are invited to shout into one of the six arms protruding from its hexagonal base and watch as their collective screams, with the help of electronic amplification, become manifest as vibrations in an adjacent tray of liquid. This totemistic sculpture parodies a number of dissonant ideas. Jenny's theory of Cymatics, the idea that all matter in the universe vibrates and therefore through its study we can gain a more complete understanding of existence, is combined with Primal Scream Therapy, a popular misreading of the natural therapy pioneered by Janov in the late 1960s that linked the repression of mental pain with physical breakdown. A third strand is presented through the introduction of Swedenborg's proposition that the original communication was a pure expression of divinity from which language was subsequently generated. This further abstracts the procedure into an investigation into the true nature of the word. The sculpture therefore functions as a multi-faceted experimental mechanism, the language of logic applied to an illogical interweaving of theories, which relies on the viewer for activation.

Titchner links disparate elements of the installation through the repetition of the hexagon, the graphic symbol for benzene which is a key solvent used in organic chemistry. This motif is further disseminated through the number six. The six vertical freestanding banners surrounding the sculpture echo in scale and form the religious standards common to churches and cathedrals (a swallow-tailed silk flag suspended from a pole). At the centre of each, a hand-carved wooden plaque is inscribed with a single word introduced by the word 'and', suggesting an infinite accumulation of information. Contrasting with the roughly hewn surface of the sculpture and acting as a sort of altarpiece for the space, a huge digitally printed banner confidently asserts BE ANGRY BUT DON'T STOP BREATHING. Its typeface is reminiscent of early computer graphics and is offset by a digitally generated starburst that is an attempt to suggest spiritual redemption and deliverance.

The phrase is taken from the poster for WR: Mysteries of the Organism, the controversial 1971 film by Dusan Makavejev loosely based on the life and work of Wilheim Reich. Found text features largely in Titchner's practice, eclectic phrases pilfered from miscellaneous sources and transformed into philosophical proclamations that seemingly demand a response. However, an ambiguity surrounds the tone of the delivery of these phrases as they are presented, devoid of context, as slick graphic posters or lightboxes with the vapidity of mainstream advertising. It is unclear whether we are to interpret them with sincerity, cynicism or humour. Titchner sees these proclamations as a sort of 'cod-philosophy, scavenged from the collapsed space that used to keep disciplines like philosophy and pop music apart'.*

Titchner does not appear to offer judgement or critique of the theories he appropriates. Rather, he provides a secular reinterpretation, maintaining a freedom to mix and overlay ideas. He exploits the catchphrases and clichés that bubble to the surface while dispensing with the theoretical frameworks from which they emerged. Through this process, he simultaneously highlights the redundancy of once radical thought whilst acknowledging the potential for certain aspects to seep quietly into popular consciousness. By amalgamating ideologies, Titchner persuades us to accept the validity of opposing beliefs, underlining both the susceptibility and complexity of the collective psyche.

Lizzie Carey-Thomas

* Mark Titchner interviewed by Mark Dickenson in *Playing amongst the ruins*, Royal College of Art, London 2001, p.90

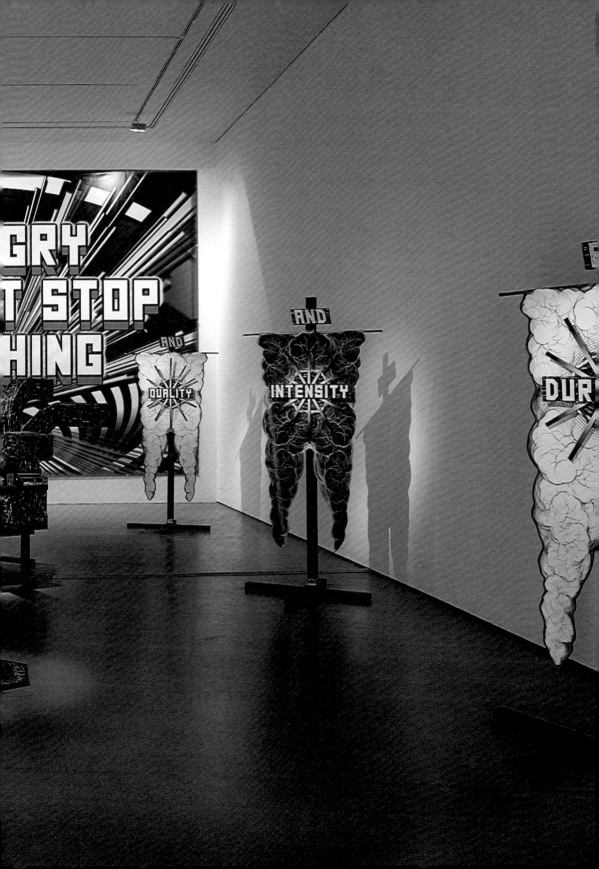

IF THE TRUTH CAN BE TOLD SO AS TO BE UNDERSTOOD IT WILL BE BELIEVED.

1. YOU ARE NOT ALONE. IN OUR SICK SOCIETY WE ARE ALL SICK.
2. THIS SICKNESS AND ITS CONSEQUENT TRAUMA IS COMPOUNDED BY THE ISOLATION OF THE INDIVIDUAL WITHIN THE TRAUMATISED WHOLE.
3. SIMPLE ACTS OF INTERACTION MAY BEGIN THE RECALIBRATION OF THIS RELATIONSHIP.
4. SO LET US BEGIN TODAY AND TOGETHER SING OUR FEARS.
5. LIBERATING OUR PRIMAL VOICE AND SHARING OUR TERROR.
6. LET US SING HUMANITY'S BIRTH SONG.
7. BY THIS ACTION WE RECALL THE VOICE THAT BECAME THE WORD.
8. THE PURE DESCRIPTION OF THE UNIVERSE THAT WE ALL CONTAIN.
9. TOGETHER IN THE QUIET MODULATION OF LIQUID WE GIVE FORM TO OUR FEARS.
10. WE ARE MATTER AND ALL MATTER VIBRATES.
11. BY THE OBSERVATION OF VIBRATION WE MAY LEARN SOMETHING OF OUR TRUE NATURE.
12. TOGETHER WE VIBRATE AND TOGETHER WE ARE ALONE.

IF THE TRUTH CAN BE TOLD SO AS TO BE UNDERSTOOD IT WILL BE BELIEVED.

1. [[YOU] EQUALS A PROPER SUBSET OF [EVERYONE]. FOR ALL ELEMENTS OF THE SET [EVERYONE], SICK EQUALS TRUE IF [ELEMENT OF [INTERSECTION [EVERYONE, SOCIETY]]] EQUALS TRUE] EQUALS A.
2. SICK IMPLIES TRAUMA IF [EXISTS ELEMENT OF THE SET INTERSECTION [EVERYONE, ISOLATED]] EQUALS B.
3. [EXISTS ELEMENT OF SET [INTERACTIONS] FOR WHICH SIMPLE EQUALS TRUE] IMPLIES NOT A AND/OR NOT B.
4. [EXISTS ELEMENT OF THE SET [EVERYONE [INTERSECTION [YOU, TODAY, SING, FEARS]]] EQUALS TRUE] EQUALS C.
5. C IMPLIES [EXISTS ELEMENT OF THE SET [EVERYONE [INTERSECTION [PRIMAL, VOICE, TERROR]]] EQUALS TRUE] EQUALS D.
6. D IMPLIES [FOR ALL ELEMENTS OF THE SET [INTERSECTION [HUMANITY, SING]], NOT [EXISTS ELEMENT OF SET [SING], OLDER EQUALS TRUE]] EQUALS E.
7. E IMPLIES [FOR ALL ELEMENTS OF THE SET [EVERYONE], VOICE EQUALS WORD].
8. EVERYONE IS A SUBSET OF EVERYTHING.
9. INTERSECTION [EVERYTHING, UNION [LIQUID, FORM, FEARS]] EQUALS QUIET MODULATION.
10. [FOR ALL ELEMENTS OF THE SET [EVERYONE], MATTER EQUALS TRUE] AND [FOR ALL ELEMENTS OF THE SET [MATTER], VIBRATE EQUALS TRUE].
11. IF [EXISTS ELEMENT OF SET [VIBRATE], OBSERVED EQUALS TRUE] IMPLIES [EXISTS ELEMENT OF SET [NATURE], TRUE EQUALS TRUE.
12. IF [UNION [VIBRATION, EVERYTHING] EQUALS TRUE] IMPLIES [YOU] EQUALS A SUBSET OF EVERYONE.

previous page
BE ANGRY BUT DON'T STOP BREATHING
2003
Courtesy the artist and Vilma Gold, London
above
detail from
BE ANGRY BUT DON'T STOP BREATHING
2003
Courtesy the artist and Vilma Gold, London

What makes a man start fires
2003
Courtesy the artist and Vilma Gold, London

David Musgrave

David Musgrave creates understated yet poignant works which demand a level of scrutiny and contemplation rarely encouraged in most forms of contemporary culture. The speculative potential of visual experience is at the very heart of Musgrave's practice, and the rewards for the viewer lie in an intellectual engagement with the games of illusion played by the artist, as well as an enjoyable aesthetic encounter. Yet the means are simple; most of the materials Musgrave uses might be supplied at primary school – paper, plasticine, graphite pencil and paint.

In works created especially for this Art Now exhibition, Musgrave uses diverse means to further his investigations into art's capacity for representation. We all share a drive to recognise the human in what we see, and he pushes this desire to its limits. His anthropomorphic forms are invariably created from an unseen original, then enlarged and translated into different media. Thus the floor sculpture, *Paper golem*, began as torn pieces of paper shuffled around until the arrangement offered just the slightest echo of a recognisable figure. This moment is frozen by translating the pieces of paper into painted aluminium, so that what might be taken at first glance to be a casual presentation is in fact a precise and meticulously made recreation. In this playful way the viewer's attention is shifted from recognising the subject to deciphering the process through which it has been created. It is at this moment that the actual subject of the work begins to emerge; its content lies not in how lifelike – or abstract – a figure is, but in the very process of working through the layers of suggestion and allusion. The actual attempt to represent, and the viewer's instinctive response to this, is what fascinates Musgrave. It is not necessarily *what* is being presented, but the cognitive process through which we recognise – or misrecognise – what is happening that offers a key to the subject of the work.

In these new works the legibility of the figure is broken down to an unprecedented level. The wall painting relates more to abstraction than figuration, the result of what Musgrave calls an attempt to 'disintegrate the figure into a gesture'. In order to get to this point, he has repeatedly torn up and repaired a paper maquette in a process he describes as 'unfolding the figure into abstraction'. Yet we are encouraged to see a human form by its title: *Giant torn tape figure (grey)*. There is no tape though, but a realistic representation of it using varying shades of silk emulsion paint. Within this completely flat, two-dimensional work the illusion of space is captured within the layers painted directly onto the wall, creating the impression that the figure is constructed from overlapping pieces of a translucent material. For Musgrave, the consistent references to something outside of the work itself – the human form, the activity of making – is vital as a way to explore both issues of representation and the complexities of a formal process. Just as the huge tape figure twists its way along the wall, so the work avoids being pinned down to any one meaning.

The way in which this piece holds the vast wall and architectural space, despite the neutrality of the colours and subtlety of line, contrasts sharply with the intense, highly reflective figure presented on the adjacent wall. This tiny object was created by squeezing paint from the tube and remodelling it in epoxy putty. Coated with a high gloss cadmium red paint this work, simply called *Painted form no.2*, has a jewel-like quality. The drawing on the opposite wall also derives from a loosely modelled figure, this time in plasticine, which is then enlarged and drawn in graphite pencil. Since Musgrave makes these drawings freehand there is a level of interpretation and therefore error. A drawing rendered realistically is inevitably slightly altered from its original image, thus entrapping the viewer in the gap between real experience and imagination.

In this deliberately pared down exhibition, each work exists independently and yet plays a supporting role to the other pieces. The wide range of media used by Musgrave allows him to experiment, at times manipulating a substance, at others allowing it to behave according to its natural properties. In a delicate balance of scale, medium and process, each work demands attention and consideration, and in taking the time, the viewer slowly unravels the exquisite tension between figuration and abstraction, identification and deception, materiality and immateriality.

Katharine Stout

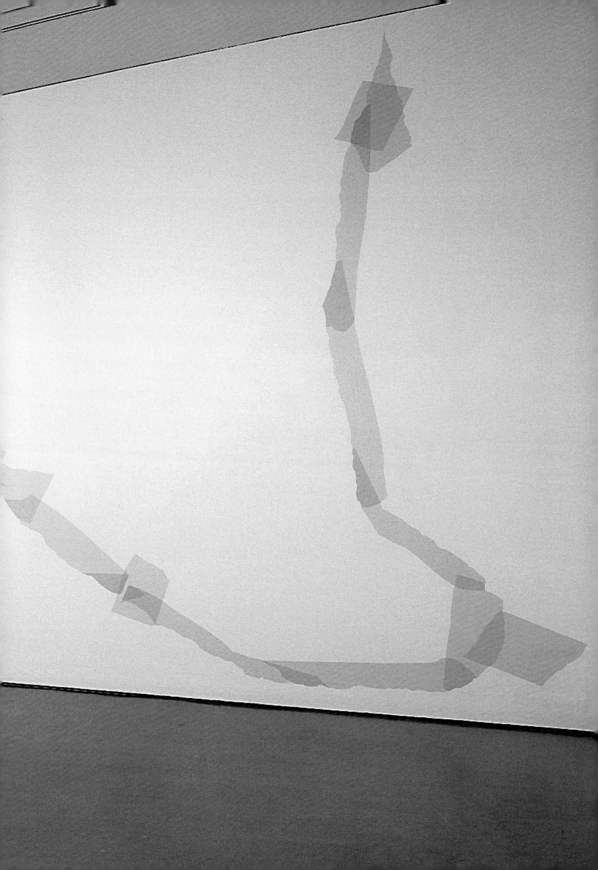

previous page background
Giant torn tape figure (grey)
2003
Courtesy the artist and greengrassi, London
previous page foreground
Paper golem
2003
Courtesy the artist and greengrassi, London
above
Paper golem
2003
Courtesy the artist and greengrassi, London

Painted form no.2
2003
Courtesy the artist and greengrassi, London

Roger Hiorns

Roger Hiorns makes works of art whose particular aesthetic lies somewhere between the representational and non-representational, and so disrupts our expectations of the boundaries between them. His sculptures have a seemingly straightforward, functional material presence, but this is always combined with an element which provides a sense of the imaginary, the poetic or the esoteric. The tension between these two aspects is a vital part of Hiorns' work.

For *Vauxhall* 2003 Hiorns has sunk a gully into the surface of the sculpture court at Tate Britain but, instead of water running down through the grating, a flame rises up from it. Gullies and gutters are usually un-noticed, part of the everyday that we encounter without needing to negotiate or consider. They have associations with particular environments. In their normal context they have a specific function which is here subverted by the artist. As he explains it 'the fire transforms the reason for the gully to exist'. Transformation is a theme throughout Hiorns' work. He has arrived at a formula which involves combining two basic elements, having found a third, or more, to be 'superfluous'. The fact that he limits himself to this structure means that we are more conscious of the relationship or dialogue between the two. They transform and disrupt each other and are often materially very different: steel and perfume (used in another work also titled *Vauxhall* 2003), steel and thistles (*Intelligence and Sacrifice* 2003) or, here, a steel grating and a flame. In each case one is entirely functional and the other something that carries with it the notion of the sacred. Furthermore, Hiorns often uses a material that transforms itself, such as copper sulphate which changes from a liquid to vivid blue crystals, or soapy liquids that bubble into foam. This element allows the sculpture to finish or conclude itself beyond the control of the artist. It also introduces chance or chaos into works which are often very formal, deliberate and resolved structures.

If Hiorns' objects look functional yet also like votive objects, they also appear familiar but totally alien, sitting in his constructed space between the representational and non-representational. The ceramic material and the forms of the vessels in works such as *Two Forms (Orange and Brown)* 1999 remind us of things that we come across everyday, but they are entirely unlike anything else that we have actually seen. The column of foaming bubbles they quietly and gently emit gives them a purpose, but also reinforces our sense of their strangeness. We cannot fit them into our ordered world of objects that have a place and a purpose.

The artist describes *Vauxhall* as 'pro-active', working both with and against its environment. The gully grating sits naturally with the architecture and landscape of the sculpture court. It could almost have always been there alongside the manholes and other functional structures, except perhaps for the fact that it sits incongruously in the centre, where a drain would never actually be placed, and at a very slightly unexpected angle, at odds with the right angles that dictate the placing of every-thing else. At the same time the work completely alters its surroundings. The flame disrupts a safe and ordered institutional space and seems unconnected with it. The fire feels unpredictable and dangerous, in total contrast to the seemingly ordered nature of its situation.

Both fire and the gutter are highly symbolic and suggestive. They allude to religion, sacred ritual and the eternal flame and conversely to dirt, ignominy, undercurrents and things hidden. As with Hiorns' other works, *Vauxhall* is potentially loaded with references whilst managing to remain elusive and un-explainable. The artist sees it as a 'proposition' open to different and personal interpretations. His role is to place the elements in an alternative context in order to provoke these readings. At the same time the work does not depend on any such associations. It has an internal logic and reason for being that is peculiar to itself. Both this logic and the object itself exist independently of anything else. The artist says that: 'The works are successful if they are self-contained and need nothing else. They exist by their own language.' It is this self-containment that is common to all Hiorns' works, however visually diverse they appear to be.

Alongside his individual, self-contained sculptural pieces, Hiorns has invented an imaginary environment or area that would provide a home for his work. This was initially conceived of as HSA – Home Space Available – a proposed social project, perhaps something like a hostelry. The artist wanted this to be a sanitised, hygienic space with suggestions of the utopian, somewhere that would be free from distraction apart from the objects in it. This later evolved into something less specific, not nec-essarily a building, but possibly a space or even just a suggestion of a certain area. He describes all of his works as containing their own clues about how this place might perform. One possible location is Vauxhall, from where this work and two other works get their title. Hiorns is interested in places that might share a particular aesthetic, places like Vauxhall that one passes through to get to somewhere else. Although the self-containment of Hiorns' works is undeniable, he is also concerned that there is an intangible area between them which is inconclusive, a place that he feels needs to be 'dealt with', often by making another work to fill the gap between existing pieces. His projected physical space may never materialise, and in fact it may not need to, but Hiorns is concerned to provide a framework for the works, which allows them to relate only to each other, and not to anything else.

Carolyn Kerr

all images
Vauxhall
2003
Courtesy the artist and Corvi-Mora, London

Lightbox 1

Breda Beban *Walk of Three Chairs* 2003
Courtesy Film and Video Umbrella and John Hansard Gallery

Breda Beban's deeply personal and evocative films confront the emotional complexity of human experience. *Walk of Three Chairs* shows Beban floating on a raft between two banks of the Danube in Belgrade, believed by some to be the point at which the Balkans end and Europe begins. One bank reveals an industrial landscape whilst the other is populated by trees

and traditional wooden dachas (country cottages). The film takes its title from a traditional Balkan pagan ritual, one that the artist recalls her grandfather performing after winning at gambling. This precarious yet celebratory act, performed by Beban against the shifting backdrop, is for her an expression of 'a complex kind of joy, joy informed by sadness'. This idea of the bittersweet is encapsulated in the love song Beban attempts to sing as she travels; *Who Doesn't Know How to Suffer Doesn't Know How to Love.*

Ann Course in collaboration with Paul Clark *Waiting for Waste* 2000; *Recruitment Video* 2000; *The Artist* 2000; *Mother* 2000; *Untitled* 1999; *Black Magic* 2003; *Shit Belt* 2000

Courtesy the artists and LUX

'Course makes visual puns on mating, parenthood and female desire. With tight understatement and humour, the images recall drawings by Nicola Tyson and Louise

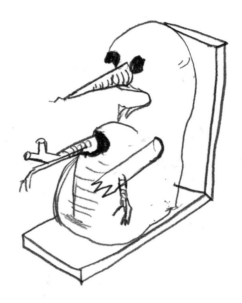

Bourgeois without feeling derivative.' Cherry Smyth

Since 1993, Ann Course and Paul Clark have collaborated on a series of short animations. Together they produce psychologically piercing films constructed from drawings on paper that are passed under a rostrum camera which has a specially mounted lens. The films are mostly edited 'in-camera' thus avoiding lavish post-production in expensive edit suites. The speed at which the two produce their animations (sometimes in a matter of hours) encourages a sense of raw energy and playfulness often lacking in more traditional animation techniques. The individual drawings, by Course, are imbued with a sharp sense of personal recollection: recurring motifs include images of coffins, penises, and holes, as well as one instance of a butterfly with wings inscribed 'mother' and 'father'. Our interpretation of the significance of these symbols is allowed to drift as the narrative becomes increasingly open-ended. We gradually realise that these drawings might have importance for ourselves as well as for the artists.

Mark Lewis *Children's Games (Heygate Estate)* 2002
Courtesy Film and Video Umbrella and Cornerhouse

Heygate Estate in south east London, a large housing development completed in 1974, was originally conceived as a self-contained community. Today this English example of pragmatic Modernism is regarded as a social and economic failure. Mark Lewis has filmed *Children's Games (Heygate Estate)* as one uninterrupted travelling shot, referring to and play-

ing with the language and grammar of film, which is a core theme in his work. The camera glides along the walkway that runs above ground throughout the estate, creating a seamless vision of the modernist structures and spaces which have systematically failed to meet the residents' needs or desires. Yet as the image drifts through the buildings the viewer gradually becomes aware of movement taking place in the background and at the periphery. Whether playing ball, flying kites, roller skating or cycling on this perfect spring day, groups of children transform the brutally defined urban areas into carefree and lively dwelling spaces, thus offering a glimpse or recollection of the original utopian dream.

Dan Holdsworth *Anechoic* 2003

Sound Design: Welburn Kispert
Courtesy the artist

In 2001 Dan Holdsworth made a series of photographs, *The Black Mountains*, in the desert-like terrain of southern Iceland; a vast black sand plain which stretches for miles between the sea and a huge glacier. The experience of being in this place was both magical

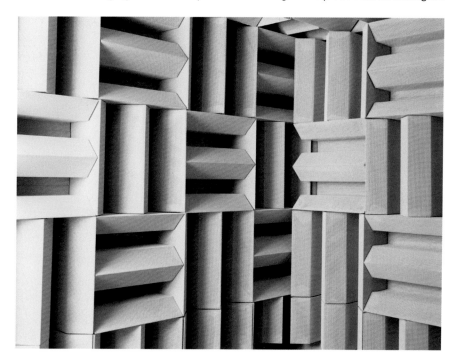

and destabilising, because of the intensity and clarity of the light and the silence. When he returned, Holdsworth became fascinated by anechoic chambers, test laboratories for sound or electrical equipment. These, in a completely man-made way, offer the same heightened physical experience: 'For me it is an experience of the techno sublime. A powerful sense of awe inspired by the product of our own human nature. A reflection of ourselves. An imprint of the human mind'. *Anechoic* is composed of different computer-manipulated images of these laboratories. These are accompanied by a sound piece comprising recordings made in an anechoic chamber by hyper sensitive microphones. The work does not recreate these environments but responds to the experience of existing in places in which boundaries are tested to the limits, whether of technology, or of the mind.

Oliver Payne & Nick Relph *Mixtape* 2002
Courtesy Gavin Brown's enterprise, New York

Mixtape takes as its starting point a recording by Terry Riley called *You're No Good*
1967. A throbbing electronic drone dramatically increases in pitch and intensity as the camera
draws back from the face of a young lad with a sparkler in his mouth. The camera moves further
away in pulses to reveal birds of prey and a floral wreath reading 'Besht Mate'. As the music

strains to breaking point, black paint runs down the walls accompanied by bursts of confetti. A
bass guitar punctuates clips of a kid garage band. A girl dances gracefully in an underpass,
observed by her crisp-eating partner. A sequence involving a bejewelled tortoise recalls
Huysmans' novel *Against Nature* while a Rastafarian beats the street with a hammer, recalling
Lee Scratch Perry's attempts to goad the devil. A line dancer – who features in an earlier work
called *House and Garage* 2000 – appears in vivid strobe-light. Images of English wildlife and
parkland deer form a backdrop to a couple necking on a sofa, only to be interrupted by unset-
tling footage of American hunt clubs shooting prey. All in all, *Mixtape* elicits a visceral response
as it careers from one surreal situation to the next.

Phil Collins *Baghdad Screentests 2002*
Courtesy Kerlin Gallery, Dublin

Phil Collins has worked in Belfast, Belgrade and Baghdad – all of them well-documented zones of civil and political unrest. Using video and photography, Collins explores the complexities of political upheaval and its impact on representation and identity. He adopts the conventions of documentary reportage, often structured around a form of portraiture or personal exchange.

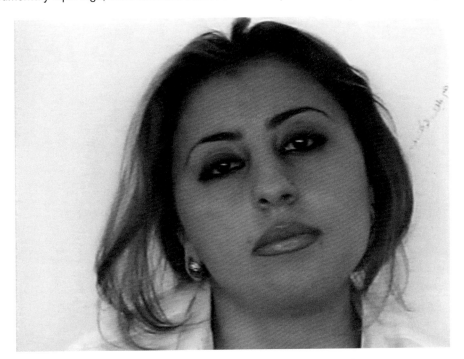

'In 2002 I travelled to Baghdad. It seemed to me that newspapers and magazines had been referring to the place for a while as an extension of the regime. Baghdad did this, they'd say. Or, Baghdad did that. So I wanted primarily to meet people. I went to colleges and visited classrooms. I told people that I was making a film and I wanted them to sit for me.' In *Baghdad Screentests* Collins invited students to participate in a Warholian style 'screen test'. A series of mesmerizing portraits emerge, accompanied by an eclectic soundtrack that includes Elvis Presley, Donna Summer and The Smiths.

Jaki Irvine *Actress* 2003

Actress: Ilaria di Luca

Courtesy the artist and Frith Street Gallery

Overheard conversations and chance incidents often provide the starting point for Jaki Irvine's work. She creates elliptical narratives, interweaving fact and fiction, drawing out the intricacies of human emotions and experiences. Shot on Super-8 and 16mm, her films often appear

to be fragments from longer narratives. *Actress* 2003 was inspired by a story that Irvine was told. It focuses on a young woman whom we see in close-up, an actress seemingly rehearsing for the camera. She appears perplexed and embarrassed, on the brink of saying something. The accented voice-over recounts her story: 'She had always wanted to be an actress. So as soon as she got the chance she went to study in Rome. After years of hard work she finally got a small part in a film. Her father was the mayor of a small town. When he heard of the film he booked a hall for one night and arranged for a copy to be sent from Rome. Finally the whole town was gathered, waiting'. At precisely this moment the actress finally speaks, she quickly says 'I have ugly breasts' and with that, the film ends.

Saskia Olde Wolbers *Placebo* 2002

Courtesy the artist and Maureen Paley / Interim Art, London

In her video works Saskia Olde Wolbers merges the virtual and the real. Drawing on stories gleaned from newspaper reports, documentaries or conversations, Olde Wolbers weaves surreal tales of human drama involving individuals who are caught in the perilous space between reality and their imaginations. These complex narratives are set against

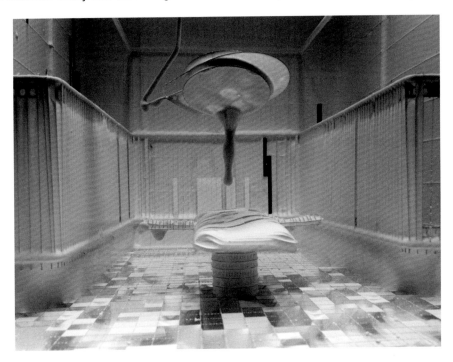

dreamlike images that appear to occupy an otherworldly territory that is both familiar and alien. The slickness of the imagery suggests computer intervention yet each scene has been meticulously constructed in the studio using low tech materials and shot on a digital video camera. *Placebo* is set in the intensive care unit of a hospital, seen from the perspective of a woman, who, lying beside her critically injured lover, discovers the hidden truth behind his web of intricately fabricated deceit. As the poignant off-camera narrative slowly unfolds, scenes of the empty ward gradually disintegrate and melt into liquid globules, mirroring the anaesthetised haze of the patient as she slips between semi-consciousness and delirium.

Lucy McKenzie

Lucy McKenzie lives and works in Glasgow, and her artistic practice is informed by the diverse creative networks that underlie and invigorate this city. When describing the current art scene there, Michael Bracewell wrote of an 'ambient artistic practice – art which occurs across all manner of pervasive media, proceeding in its own way at its own pace' and he clearly had McKenzie in mind. She creates, curates and collaborates, questioning our expectations of how art should operate.

Not long after she graduated from Duncan of Jordanstone College, McKenzie won acclaim for her work. With a deft but knowing hand, she would inter-weave iconic images and styles from art history with the fabric of popular culture. Her ability to re-contextualise the past in the present was no doubt partly due to her experiences in Glasgow – a city with a rich and colourful history that has been substantially redeveloped and rebuilt in recent years.

McKenzie is continually testing out different media and disciplines, as she showed in her exhibition for Art Now. The title of the project, *MMIV*, referred to the year ahead, and the show was a subtle enquiry into the nature of artistic identity and art production. McKenzie presented a film that had been edited from footage of a performance with the Gdansk artist Paulina Olowska. In this piece, entitled *Hold The Colour*, McKenzie and Olowska had self-consciously adopted the caricatured roles of 'working women' – an artist and an architect respectively – and created an intriguing narrative that explored the idea of art-making, its process and context, and its reception. In front of a minimal but highly formal set, each woman appeared on stage separately, although their physical similarities implied they were mirror images of one another. When they did appear together, McKenzie began to sketch Olowska's portrait. McKenzie swiftly drew an outline of Olowska's face. As the artist, McKenzie was demonstrating to us her ability to translate what was in front of her into a work of art. Art's transformation of reality was a central theme of the performance. The stilted poses and gestures of both protagonists only added to the air of contrivance. This was reiterated by the fact that the performance had now been made into an edited film, with the addition of an icy, melancholic piano score strengthening the sense of artifice.

It was this atmospheric soundtrack that any visitor to the Art Now space would have heard first. At times it set the nerves on edge. The gallery was divided into two rooms, and the actual film was not immediately visible. In the first space, McKenzie presented prints and drawings. Two of these depicted Glasgow cityscapes, *View from Oxford Street, Glasgow 1980* and *View to Ballater Street, Glasgow 1980*, their stark and rectilinear forms rendered in minimal monochrome. These images were based on photographic reproductions that McKenzie had found, and although they dated from only two decades ago their Spartan austerity was a reminder of how much the city had changed. The views were also reminiscent of former Eastern European cityscapes, with the silhouetted buildings of the lino print appearing close to abstraction. The works flanked McKenzie's handmade silkscreen year-planner for 2004 (*MMIV*) which was placed centrally on one wall, pinned very simply to it. The year planner remained exquisitely blank, emblematic of the artist as a 'cultural worker', alone in the studio: planning, working and of course waiting.

Viewed in its entirety the exhibition gave off the impression of an uncompromising austerity, perhaps not what everyone might have expected. McKenzie was ever-mindful of what it meant to make this exhibition within the context of Tate Britain in London and the works that she presented here posed a number of pertinent questions. Tate, like many cultural institutions in recent years, has a powerful and persuasive branding strategy. For a young artist – for any artist – the prospect of engaging with such mechanisms is loaded with difficulties. McKenzie is an astute critic of the way culture and heritage has become so packaged. Her interest in the role of artists today, and her questioning of the meaning and purpose of art-making, naturally leads her to examine the systems of patronage that promote and support it. Tate is a registered charity, but whilst making a show here McKenzie chose to highlight the activities of another charitable organisation, one which was in fact based in Poland and had received considerably less publicity and support. It is called La Strada and McKenzie painted its bold red-and-black logo on the wall that led into the exhibition space, mounted information about its activities and interests alongside it, and invited visitors to take away photocopied sheets. Supplies were constantly running out, such was the demand. Moreover, McKenzie made it known that if any of the works she had made for this project were sold, she would donate her share to La Strada.

La Strada raises awareness about, and fights against, the illegal trafficking of women in Poland, lobbying for support from the government and the public. Being caught between the wealthy countries of the European Union and the poverty of Belarus and the Ukraine, Poland is particularly vulnerable, and has experienced a great influx of migrants since the late 1980s. Having spent time in Poland in recent years and through her contact with Olowska, McKenzie was conscious of this growing problem and chose to draw attention to it, thus adding another layer to her project.

McKenzie actively probes the meaning and significance of socially engaged art, and how artists today can and do relate to the wider world. She wove together a number of different ideas and interests, setting off conversations, asking a lot of poignant questions, and created space to think as well as see.

Mary Horlock

installation view
La Strada

still from
Oblique Composition
2003
Made in collaboration with Paulina Olowska
Courtesy the artist and Cabinet, London

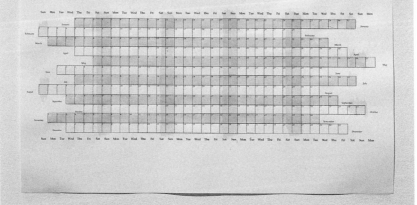

MMIV
2003
Courtesy the artist and Cabinet, London

installation view (clockwise from left)
View from Oxford Street, Glasgow 1980
2003
Courtesy the artist and Cabinet, London
View to Ballater Street, Glasgow 1980
2003
Courtesy the artist and Cabinet, London

Ian Kiaer

An inattentive viewer could overlook Ian Kiaer's groupings of architectural models, found objects, paintings and drawings arranged modestly on and around the gallery floor. Yet the rudimentary nature of his materials – a block of polystyrene, an upturned plastic bin – contrasts directly with the epic subjects they evoke – a snow-covered sweep of land, a vertical cliff face – while painted backdrops lend spatial depth and context to the settings. Each component acts as a visual notation to a complex, fragmentary narrative, derived from Kiaer's comprehensive research into the idealistic notions of various eccentric visionaries. Whether architect, philosopher or artist, each is united across history in their search for a retreat from the dominant ideologies of their day or concerned with methods for the physical or social integration of man and environment. Emblematic of unrealised or abandoned utopias, Kiaer's works are inevitably imbued with a wistful romance, whose transience is eloquently articulated through the ephemeral materials used.

For Art Now, Kiaer brings together two ongoing projects inspired by the landscape paintings of the sixteenth-century artist Pieter Brueghel and the working spaces of the philosopher Ludwig Wittgenstein. He presents earlier works alongside new pieces that develop previously established themes. Tentative connections weave through the works: the desire to view the world from a remote position, and the importance attributed to the location of the workplace or studio within the landscape, whether imaginary or built. However, rather than illustrate specific narratives, Kiaer evokes a context in which ideas and motifs overlap, encouraging a dialogue between the disparate components.

In *Brueghel project / Casa Malaparte* 1999 Kiaer links Brueghel with the Italian poet Curzio Malaparte, who was exiled by Mussolini in 1933 to the same mountainous and remote part of Italy that the painter had journeyed through several centuries earlier. The work comprises a large, battered chunk of blue foam, positioned next to a stool. On the stool is a smaller square of brown foam supporting a tiny balsa wood house, suggesting an isolated dwelling dwarfed by its surroundings. On the wall hangs a canvas painted with an empty landscape, its only feature a windmill situated precariously on top of a mountain. Kiaer has taken the windmill motif from Brueghel's *The Procession of Calvary* and draws parallels to the retreat Malaparte was inspired to build on a rocky promontory above the Tyrrhenian Sea following his two and a half years of isolation.

The theme of artistic pursuit resulting from voluntary or enforced exile is central to the installation and unites many of Kiaer's earlier works. *Wittgenstein project / palm house* 2002 and *Wittgenstein project / Skjolden* 2003 refer to the remote buildings where the philosopher worked in Ireland and Norway respectively. The latter takes as its focus the small wooden house of vernacular Norwegian design that the philosopher commissioned to be built in 1913. Overlooking a lake and surrounded by cliffs, it provided Wittgenstein with the almost hermetic conditions he needed to work on *Tractatus Logico Philosophicus*. Kiaer's work consists of an overturned kitchen waste bin, a small pink watercolour and strips of pink Styrofoam lying horizontally on the floor. The colour guides our reading of the objects as part of a unified landscape and, for Kiaer, is indicative of the romantic nature of Wittgenstein himself.

The viewer cannot hope to grasp all the intricate associations that permeate Kiaer's compositions. The links he makes are intuitive rather than academic; by layering references and leaping across centuries Kiaer generates relationships between complex ideas and individuals. Yet while his motives remain multi-faceted, the arrangements retain a visual coherence that captures a sense of the subject. Constituent parts of a composition are often fused through tone and colour. *Brueghel project /studio* refers to Brueghel's painting *Winter*, and an impression of desolate chill is evoked through the use of grey/green tinged props. The cardboard model with acetate window relates to a building designed by contemporary architects Anne Lacaton and Jean-Phillipe Vassal in 1993, a sort of 'archetypal studio', half enclosed and half exposed to the external landscape. The use of the model in Kiaer's compositions has connotations of the 'ideal', yet also suggests a project still to be realised, existing only in the imagination. Furthermore, in *Brueghel project /studio* Kiaer highlights the impracticality of such a design by situating it in an inappropriately hostile climate.

Kiaer gives form to select visions whilst simultaneously emphasising their remoteness from reality. The painted backdrops indicate the projected ideal while the impoverished props represent the transient and unattainable nature of such ambitions. At once merged into and overwhelmed by the cavernous expanse of the gallery, the tableaux operate as miniature theatre, drawing us in, yet, never allowing us to engage fully with the fantasy. Balanced precariously between imagined and real spaces, Kiaer's works exist on the periphery, encapsulating the disparity between art and life.

Lizzie Carey-Thomas

detail from
Brueghel project / Casa Malaparte
1999
Private collection, London

previous page
installation view (clockwise from left)
Brueghel project / Casa Malaparte
1999
Private collection, London
Brueghel project / studio
2003
Collection of Marina Pichler, Milan
Courtesy Alison Jaques Gallery, London
Wittgenstein project / Skjolden
2003
Collection of Ann and Marshall Webb, Toronto
Courtesy Alison Jaques Gallery, London
above
Brueghel project / studio
2003
Collection of Marina Pichler, Milan
Courtesy Alison Jaques Gallery, London

Lightbox 2

Daria Martin *Birds* 2001

Birds 2001 playfully recalls the simple abstract performances of the 1920s Bauhaus choreographer Oskar Schlemmer, in which he explores the presence of the human figure in space through the use of striking costumes and props. In Martin's witty version for the twenty-first century, actors preen in costumes made from low-tech, everyday materials and form a series

of still tableaux for the constantly circling camera. The five dancers hold poses against a home-made theatrical set, which is continually moving around them. Delicate lighting and a quietly haunting soundtrack created on a Moog synthesizer suggest a serene, even romantic mood as the viewer is allowed a glimpse into the illusory and private world of these performing 'birds'.

Martin says of her films, 'The opposite of overbudgeted Hollywood blockbusters, my films are like magic acts that show how the trick is done ...'. She describes the world she depicts as 'a shifting, sometimes humorous realm of desire where images glide, change, transform, physically as well as mentally – oscillating between the intimately linked impulses of romanticism and disillusionment'. *Birds* explores a continual flux between stasis and movement. Changing details such as a piece of cellophane held against a dancer's face, or a roughly painted paper sleeve held together with coloured tape celebrate the power of colour and form. The work also suggests a bodily presence within abstraction – the formal language of the performance means the dancers create a parity with the objects around them.

Katy Dove *I'm so Ashamed* 2001; *Melodia* 2002, background watercolour by the artist's grandfather George Wilson, music *I kut* by Jorg Maria Zeger, published on the sampler 'colour and pattern', apestaartje 2002; *You* 2003, produced for Zenomap for the 2003 Venice Biennale, funded by the Scottish Arts Council and the British Council.

The animations of Glasgow-based artist Katy Dove are poised between abstraction

and figuration, with image and sound delicately balanced to develop or dissolve in tandem. Shifting psychedelic shapes glide lyrically across the screen, nestling together in synchronised harmony or unfurling and drifting off into the ether. Hand drawn in felt-tip and brought to life on computer, Dove's images do not so much dance to the manipulated soundtracks as give them visual form and personality.

Dove comments 'much of my work takes the form of a psychological representation of an idea, an emotion, a perception or situation. Animation has been used as a tool for exploring various psychological states from the melancholic to the frenetic'. Intricate forms spin in and out of sight leaving kaleidoscopic vapour trails in *I'm so Ashamed*. A watercolour landscape by Dove's grandfather forms the backdrop to *Melodia*, providing a tranquil setting in which birdlike forms swoop and hover, settling from time to time in the sponge-like trees. *You* follows a trajectory from day to night, accompanied by a mesmeric soundtrack featuring slowed down and remixed birdsong recordings.

Haluk Akakçe *Birth of Art* 2003

Soundtrack: Michael Vecchio

Courtesy the artist and Cosmic Galerie, Paris

Haluk Akakçe trained as an architect and began his artistic career as a painter, and both these disciplines now inform his work in digital media. In his multi- and single screen video installations, Akakçe quite literally builds another world for the viewer to escape into.

The artist describes *Birth of Art* as 'an abstract choreography using natural forms'. It is a work composed of two distinct movements: in the first, ghostly semi-figurative forms fall and flicker across a black screen, gradually dissolving the dark void. 'Like nature falling from heaven', these elements build up to create a new, light-filled space. In the second part of the film, these same forms float above a new, more hard-edged, man-made world. Here, the physical environment suggests a religious interior, such as a church, synagogue or mosque; a unique space that is public and yet dedicated to private contemplation. Akakçe's fluid forms envelope us in a strange, other reality where meanings are never fixed. He suggests that this work was inspired by the state of humanity today, struggling to find meaning through religion. Perhaps significantly, the volumetric forms in the second sequence have a hard, reflective shell-like exterior but swell and unfurl as if trying to merge with their environment.

Rob Kennedy & Stuart McGregor *You're not blank* 2002

music by *Un Caddie Renverse dans L'herbe* (remixing Janek Schaefer),
commissioned by Shadazz for the compilation 'Evil Eye is Source'
Courtesy the artists

You're not blank, a collaboration by Rob Kennedy and Stuart McGregor, uses the medium of video to explore the complex interaction between sound and image. The work was

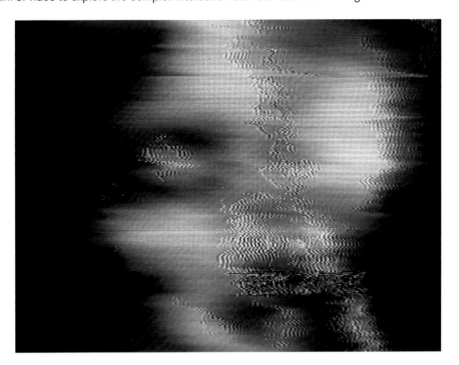

commissioned by Shadazz (a Glasgow-based multi-media label) for 'Evil Eye is Source', a compilation of collaborative videos between artists and musicians curated by artist Luke Fowler.

Pop music and its accompanying promotional videos have both been subjected to endless duplication. In *You're not blank* a video recording has been repeatedly re-duplicated in order to render the image almost non-existent. All that is left are flashes of white over a black screen, punctuated by sparks and fissures, and intermittent glimpses of a ghostly human image.

'As snow and hiss spit from the screen an image fizzes to life; this is VHS on its last legs, the tape heads still sucking the dregs of its energy. Stretched and worn the tape shoots spasms of light into retching bodies then splutters fitfully into black. This is the end; now digitally held in looping senility.' This visual unravelling is accompanied by the music of *Un Caddie Renverse dans L'herbe*, a remix of audio experiments by sound artist Janek Shaefer. The result is an audio visual breakdown analogous to the kind of neural breakdown that can be induced by watching the film continuously.

Nigel Cooke

Nigel Cooke's paintings oscillate between extremes – he works on an epic scale but dwells on the minutiae of decay and dissolution, he paints with scientific accuracy but creates scenes that could never exist. Each canvas is composed with consummate skill but offers a less than reassuring encounter with entropy and excess. Thus, his paintings seem determined to short-circuit themselves, as if bent on self-destruction.

These grand canvases betray Cooke's anxious preoccupation with the heroic ambitions of artists of the past, invoking a tradition of landscape painting which celebrated the sublime power of space. Cooke knows that such visions could inspire awe, and in both form and content his own works aspire to involve and overwhelm the viewer much as those vast historic landscapes of the nineteenth century did. But Cooke's landscapes are dismal and dysfunctional, bile-coloured, littered with derelict buildings and burnt out cars, skulls and locusts. They are unlike any other landscape portrayed by an artist working today, and they cannot be described without resorting to hyperbole. Nature is depicted as a virulent force, sometimes morphing into skull-like shapes, spiralling out of control, forcing its way through cracks and crevices. Conversely, many of Cooke's landscapes seem 'anti-nature', and the expanse of the picture plane is bare, suffused in ultraviolet hues. Their corners are scarred with menacing graffiti and the ground cluttered with Halloween pumpkins, bones, severed heads and other paraphernalia derived from the classic and kitsch iconography of popular horror movies. The associations are universally unwholesome and sinister – decrepit, decaying and heavily clichéd – allowing Cooke to devise a kind of tragic-comic melodrama within each work.

Cooke's images are meticulously painted, but this does not make their content any easier to absorb. As they crowd together in the Art Now room at Tate Britain, they inevitably produce a sense of anxiety and claustrophobia. Cooke's intention is to unsettle us. His technical mastery is undeniable, but it seems that this skill is consistently put to mis-use. His choice of imagery, and his rendering of it, is self-consciously over-wrought. Thus our awe at his creation is undermined by a sense of bathos. The artist is more than aware of this, and the fact that a barren and ruined landscape is given such a seemingly incongruous title as *Ghost on the Happy Trails* substantiates this, adding an ironic twist of country-and-western music into the toxic cocktail.

Cooke prefers a shallow picture plane: there is little, if any, depth to the paintings. Each composition is usually anchored by a narrow horizontal base line. It is along this lower band that most of the detritus is gathered: the wrecked cars, the tree stumps, the cigarette butts, the rubble. In *Ghost on the Happy Trails* the larger expanse of the canvas describes a concrete wall (or it could be an overcast sky), its yellowish tones pierced by a rainbow-like arch of golden light (or equally a stream of urine). In contrast, a work such as *Silva Morosa* portrays nature creeping across and animating the whole surface of the canvas. A skull-like apparition is summoned from the few gaps left at the centre. In another gap, high in the left corner, a tiny face stares out, and on closer inspection other pairs of eyes can be found. Cooke's human heads are a disconcerting addition: they return the viewer's gaze but communicate very little. From a distance, they easily become lost within the vast field of the painting, and since the canvas is hung so close to the floor they are more difficult to identify. The graffiti that is scrawled across the walls is yet another possible indication of human life, evidence of the humanisation and indeed personalisation of the terrain, but also a sign of protest and disorder. Of course, the graffiti is illegible, communicating no message to us, and so again our expectations are confused. The graffiti, like other aspects of the imagery Cooke uses, makes a link to the modern graphic novel or the popular comic book. Sitting at the intersection of literature and art, blending satire and caricature, the graphic novel perhaps finds a strange equivalence with some of Cooke's imaginings.

It is no surprise that Cooke wears surgeon's goggles to ensure the accuracy and clarity of his minute imagery. This means even microscopic details both bear up to and demand close scrutiny. Of course, this again undermines or contradicts the paintings' grandeur and magnitude. So much information is compressed into even these details (or 'wormholes' as Cooke calls them) that it is impossible to take everything in at once. Cooke does not allow a painting to offer itself as an all-in-one entity, where its entire scale and the material handling of its details can be comprehended from a single viewpoint. He proposes that painting can and should be a multi-layered experience: the expressive power of tiny details pulls the spectator in, but then becomes magically invisible when we stand back from the canvas. Our visual experience is thus continually in flux, and we must keep moving to comprehend one order of magnitude over another. This can be frustrating.

So much is crammed into any one of Cooke's canvases they are exhaustive and exhausting. In his mesmerising, phantasmagoric view of the world, the artist demonstrates the great chasms between realism and reality, between history and myth. Cooke endeavours to plot a course for painting that, in his own words, 'shakes off the closure of its own historical death', and by doing so he has given it an extremely perplexing after-life.

Mary Horlock

detail from
Mirrors
2003
Tate

Muntean/Rosenblum
It Is Never Facts That Tell

Muntean/Rosenblum's work appropriates adolescent figures from fashion or lifestyle magazines, transforming them into strangely compelling scenes which question the possibility of spirituality in contemporary society. Transferred to paintings, drawings and photographs, the affected stances of these youthful models echo the lines 'She's over bored, And self assured' from the cult anthem *Smells Like Teen Spirit* by Nirvana. Yet behind their studied masks, the figures are full of latent emotions they dare not express: fear, longing, desire and despair. At the core of Muntean/Rosenblum's practice is what Markus Muntean calls 'precise ambiguity'. They explore contradictions inherent in the construction of identity and the contemporary notion of self, in works which simultaneously convey absolute banality and spiritual pathos.

Adi Rosenblum comments, 'We are fascinated by, and investigate, how far you can go with the construction of the gesture of the figure. Because, we think the more artificial it gets, the more moving it is, even though, in the normal sense it is the natural that is the thing that moves you'. The archetypal static poses of these contrived figures are familiar from both contemporary popular culture and art history. Reminiscent of characters from Renaissance paintings undergoing a sublime religious experience, they reflect Christian iconography, much of which refers back to Classical art. Yet the only God you imagine these teenagers to follow would be the idols of Carhartt, Converse, Nike, Nokia, Stussy…and so on. Muntean/Rosenblum are following a tradition of figurative painting, calculated to give 'a certain aura and emotional impact'. But the desolate urban settings seem to negate the possibility of genuine emotion, leaving the viewer with an overwhelming impression of contemporary ennui.

Though Muntean/Rosenblum work in a variety of media, their practice stems from painting. They have been working in partnership since 1992 and have developed a unique joint signature style. Muntean comments, 'This double authorship has the same function as the white frame or margins, which puts the painting into brackets. These white frames or margins of course have connotations in terms of comics or TV monitors. They allow us to deal with very painterly issues and iconographies, and questions of authorship'. The appropriation of a classical language for their painting distances the treatment of the figures by the artists from the original photographic source material.

Underneath these theatrical scenes run seemingly sophisticated texts which take us by surprise in their sincerity. As in comic art, or film subtitles, we expect the words to be explanatory, yet these disjointed phrases are simply placed alongside, relevant to the image only if we choose them to be. The statements appear to offer poignant commentary on contemporary existence, for example, 'the certainty that humanity is marching towards a better earthly existence and that a radiant future is just on the horizon. This is well, kind of, mantra of modernism'. These lines of wisdom have also been literally cut and pasted from printed material, found phrases which have the semblance of philosophical statements, but when analysed are revealed to be nothing but jargon.

Somehow we expect the intimate medium of drawing to be characteristic of the individual hand of the artist, yet here the two hands are indistinguishable. The large-scale photographs on view at Gloucester Road tube station present a mise en scene for portrait drawings of teenage fashion models, which lie casually amongst the personal detritus of an artist's studio. Once again this is a deliberate ploy by the artists to set up an artificial framework that questions notions of subjectivity. In other recent small scale drawings, Muntean/Rosenblum have turned to the language of Russian Constructivist graphics for inspiration with its bold colours and strong forms, finding to their surprise that it is already a strong influence in many contemporary lifestyle and fashion magazines. By referring to such a readily identifiable historic style they take on the political associations of this idealistic movement. An installation of a number of these works, juxtaposed with the portrait drawings, highlights how even the most revolutionary of art movements can be subsumed by mass consumerism, commenting on the futility of utopianism.

A video work, *It Is Never Facts That Tell*, made specially for Art Now, takes further the idea of a dystopian vision. The bleak natural landscape, tainted with the intrusive signs of human civilization, contrasts sharply with the emotive classical music. The nostalgic mood of the film, shot in black and white, evokes the lost idealism of a bygone era. The protagonists of the film, the same good-looking young people in trendy outfits who inhabit Muntean/Rosenblum's paintings and drawings, act out their roles as protesters in a half-hearted manner. They listlessly march along holding banners with cut-out slogans, aware that ultimately their actions will have little effect.

The bold shapes of another new sculptural work, *At The Beginning...*, also refer to the Constructivist movement. Two arrows direct the viewer around the space, connecting the different elements of the exhibition. The work also offers a resting point, somewhere to stop and contemplate the drawings and paintings on the walls. The phrase printed on the tall flag at the centre point of this three-dimensional work continually defers resolution to the questions raised by the images and text presented in the exhibition: 'At the beginning we felt like we could change the world, but something happened, then something happened then something happened because something else happened'.

Though their work takes many different forms, Muntean/Rosenblum consistently explore universal themes. Collectively these striking works speak of the way in which longing for individual identity is often expressed through generic codes of fashion and behaviour promoted through the mass media. Ultimately the meaning of the works can never be pinned down, their ambiguity echoing the dilemmas of contemporary society.

Katharine Stout

installation view
Exhibition at Gloucester Road Underground Station
22 April – 19 July 2004
Courtesy Platform for Art, London Underground

Claire Barclay
Half-Light

Claire Barclay's sculptural installations balance elements of function and dysfunction, chaos and order, in a precarious equilibrium. Her work pivots around the physical and psychological tensions set up between contrasting components, pitching the organic against the synthetic, the hard against the soft, openness against confinement.

Barclay's carefully composed environments comprise multiple elements which often respond directly to the specifics of a given space. They combine hand-crafted objects with those manufactured to her own specifications and more improvisatory elements constructed in situ. Objects are grouped and regrouped from one installation to the next; Barclay views each exhibition as a 'pause' in her ongoing project refining and adding to a growing vocabulary of forms. These hybrid objects often suggest a particular function or allude to anthropomorphic or natural forms, yet remain elusive through their careful displacement. This sense of uncertainty is enhanced as the viewer navigates the installation; multiple references unfold gradually over time ensuring that meaning is perpetually evolving and mutating. Barclay uses this 'area of confusion' to investigate the complex, shifting and often contradictory relationships between people and their environments and the links between nature, culture and the commodified world.

Exploiting the physical properties of her chosen materials – leather, canvas, metal, rubber or fur, for example – to full effect, Barclay encourages us to engage with her work on a profoundly instinctual level. Invariably, an object's form and context within the installation combine to trigger a widening range of associations, veering from the domestic and utilitarian to the fetishistic.

The process of making lies at the core of Barclay's practice. By adopting methods associated with traditional crafts, such as weaving or wood turning, she investigates how experience can be communicated through form, responding intuitively to materials and embracing elements of risk and experimentation. These traits are often evident in the finished work, which can be poised between making and unmaking; fraying wicker and dangling threads suggest that process is more important than product.

Aside from such formal concerns, Barclay's interest in craft stems from its affinity to both the functional and the decorative, and the position it now occupies in a culture of mass production. New Age paraphernalia has become a recurring motif in her work; dream catchers, crystals, and other objects that purport to hold mystic or spiritual properties but are now intensively-marketed commodities. Barclay is fascinated by the contradiction inherent in a profit-led industry producing facsimile 'craft' objects aspiring to non-commercial values, and our ability to buy into different lifestyles through their acquisition. Similarly, her interest in objects that convey our ambiguous relationship to nature has led her to reference the tools of hunting which, like craft, has become a fetishised and marketed hobby quite detached from its origins.

Half-light, Barclay's project for Art Now, consists of separate zones, each linked through the loose metaphor of the owl while maintaining their autonomy. Steeped in mythology and a cipher of contradictory beliefs, this predatory creature has variously been associated with wisdom and death, good fortune and witchcraft.

As you enter the space, two floor-based structures impede your passage. Taking their titles from a type of tension-based animal trap, *Deadfall 1* and *2* are reminiscent of defunct gymnasium apparatus, manmade surrogates for natural forms. In the first a heavy bar rests on two spindly, tapering legs of differing lengths, creating a distorted tripod shape as if slumping under its weight. The second structure leans into the corner of the room, a thin metal pole with a black leather sleeve attached to its summit acting as both protection and support to a heavier bar. The slit leather strains visibly under the bar's weight, and appears ready to collapse at any moment.

In the centre of the space, two machined metal hoops are suspended side by side; a halo of thick bristle protrudes from a groove in the outer circumference of each. At the point of their intersection the bristle thrusts forward, creating an owl-like mask and forcing the industrial materials to behave in an organic fashion. The double circle motif is repeated by the two open-ended wooden cylinders positioned side by side on the floor at the far end of the space. Constructed from planks of Douglas Fir the cylinders are roughly hewn on the exterior while sanded and invitingly smooth inside. At one and a half metres in length and diameter, they relate directly to human proportions, encouraging us to bend down and mentally project ourselves inside. Barclay's use of red leather in the interior further enhances the den-like quality and the separation between inside and outside, suggesting that we are looking into something's, or someone's, psyche. Fixed to the wall and only visible in close proximity, the final element of the installation is a small stainless steel spike that has been slit down the middle and prised apart creating a sharp beak-like form.

Through the juxtaposition of elements of shelter and protection with those of capture and entrapment, Barclay creates a seductive environment charged with an undertone of threat. Her installations operate as a sort of hallucinogenic reflection of the world around us, reliant on the literal and metaphorical references we bring to them while hovering just beyond our realm of experience. Barclay not only acknowledges the power of form and material to communicate on a visual level without recourse to language but also recognises that she is as seduced by as she is sceptical about the commodified world. This duality of emotion underpins her work and perhaps explains her ability to engage so convincingly with the associative properties of her materials. By exploring the slippage between one thing and another, Barclay reveals that meaning is always in motion and impossible to harness.

Lizzie Carey-Thomas

previous page
installation view
Half-light
2004
Courtesy the artist and doggerfisher, Edinburgh
above
Sharp Dusk
2004
Courtesy the artist and doggerfisher, Edinburgh

installation view (clockwise from left)
Deadfall 1
2004
Courtesy the artist and doggerfisher, Edinburgh
Askance
2004
Courtesy the artist and doggerfisher, Edinburgh
Deadfall 2
2004
Courtesy the artist and doggerfisher, Edinburgh

Lightbox 3

Rosalind Nashashibi *Hreash House* 2004
Courtesy the artist

Rosalind Nashashibi's compelling film observes everyday life in the Hreash household. This large extended family, made up of three generations, lives in one building on the edge of Nazareth, a town that has an entirely Palestinian population though it lies in the heart of Israel.

The film documents these numerous inhabitants going about their daily lives, preparing and sharing meals, relaxing in front of the television, caring together for their children.

Sumptuous close-ups of the richly-patterned furnishings and elaborate meals show a life filled with colour and light. The camera also pans back to present a more general overview, allowing us a glimpse of Palestinian life which differs radically from the perpetual violence and suffering so often shown on television news footage.

Hreash House presents a lifestyle which seems quite alien to the compact Western family unit. It is closer to the old idea of a family as a tribe, and as Nashashibi points out, 'the family is a community in itself rather than part of a community'. Although the Hreash family members have all the visible aspects of modern life – mobile phones, children's games and diversity of dress – theirs is a way of life which is dying out.

The film emphasises direct observation, and as such does not offer any overt commentary. The world outside of the Hreash household is not represented and so the film itself gives little indication of where the family might live and their nationality. Nonetheless, the context of the work provides a thought-provoking and lasting question as to whether our understanding of an entire nation is determined by the images presented to us by the media.

Paul Morrison *Satellite* 2004

Courtesy the artist and Alison Jacques Gallery, London

Satellite is Paul Morrison's third film and continues his exploration of the natural landscape, its representation and perception in the collective consciousness. He is known as a painter, creating evocative landscape panoramas that often fill entire galleries. In all his painted works, he condenses a rich array of imagery into strikingly minimal silhouettes, using a range of sources, both historic and contemporary, playing with scale and eliminating

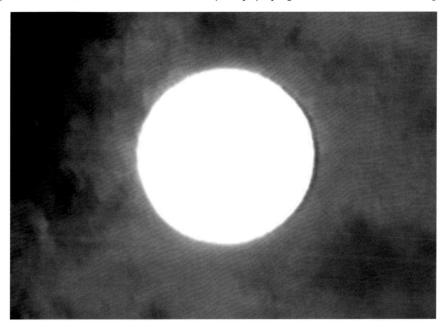

specifics. It is through such means that he has created what he calls 'cognitive landscape', an idea of landscape that we instantly recognise but that we realise is constructed, and indeed quite 'unreal'. Morrison began making films in 2002, and his working processes are worthy of comparison to his painterly technique.

Satellite has the same stripped-down, intense quality as his paintings, made more powerful by the swift edits and sharp contrasts. This film takes its imagery from existing sources, modifying film footage from disparate genres and periods to creating a shimmering, shifting montage.

Against an eerie soundtrack of whistling wind, different scenes unfurl: the view across an expanse of water cuts to a journey down-river with a mountainous landscape perfectly reflected in the surface of the water. Scale and distance quickly collapse, as one image merges seamlessly into another. Our viewpoint shifts with it: one minute we crouch down low scrutinising undergrowth, the next we are looking up at trees silhouetted against the sky or clouds eclipsing a full moon. Landscape comes alive, growing and mutating before our eyes.

John Wood and Paul Harrison *66.86m* 2003

1km 2004 (funded by Arts Council England, South West)

100 m 2004

Courtesy the artists and fa projects, London

John Wood and Paul Harrison have been collaborating since 1993, creating beguiling video works that are characterised by their wit and economy of execution. The artists themselves often appear in their videos, engaging in succinct, if seemingly eccentric activities.

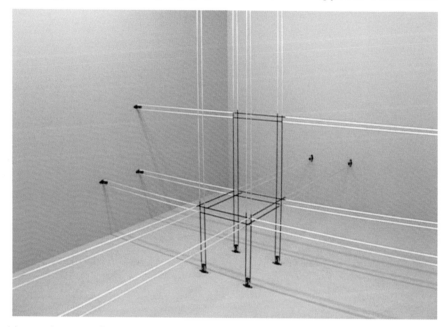

They combine sculpture and performance to explore the intriguing possibilities that might be generated from carefully staged and precisely articulated events and actions.

Wood and Harrison have created new works for Art Now Lightbox, each of them drawing lines in and across space. Shown in sequence, these videos explore the relationship between length in terms of distance and length in terms of duration, and blur the boundaries between two, three and four dimensions.

In the first video, *66.86 m*, a rope is being pulled through an elaborate system of pulleys until all the black sections meet to conjure the image of a chair. The title refers to the length of the rope. The next piece, *1km*, shows Harrison holding a belt sander over a pile of papers. As the belt turns the sheets arch into the air. Placed end to end the papers would make one kilometre, but the length is never realised, ending up in a shapeless pile on the floor.

In the final work, *100m*, a fishing line wrapped around a wooden board is wound into a ceiling fan, making the board jump violently. Here, the title refers to the length of the line. Indeed, each film takes its title from the length of its critical element.

Afterword

Looking back at the series of Art Now projects over the past eighteen months, there is a temptation to falsely identify a neat rationale behind our choice of artists. Conducting our initial research, we tried to respond openly and directly to the work we saw during each studio visit, whether it was finished, in development, or in conception. What we sought above all was diversity. We were excited and motivated by the energy of the work not only by the selected artists but in all of the studios we visited. However the final selection was often dictated by timing – what seemed right for the balance of the programme, for the development of the work and the appropriate moment in an artist's career. Though many of the artists found themselves tackling the additional pressures that come with an emerging practice – financial and time constraints, and managing their relationship with an institution – the work made for Art Now has been consistently challenging, bold, complex and original.

Now, after a year of discussions and further studio visits, the shared concerns of the artists selected are hard to miss and are explored in more detail below. These may well have influenced some of our choices, but we have no desire to identify a new group or 'ism'. Such artificial constructs tend only to confine. A fascination with materials is evident, to differing degrees, in all of the work. This engagement with materiality is allied to a rigorous enquiry into the ideas that shape content. These artists engage with the past, appropriating from an eclectic range of sources, yet their work is firmly rooted in the present.

Many of the artists have not confined themselves to one medium but move freely between a range of strategies and materials, putting physical and phenomenological experience at the forefront of their practice. The work is as much about colour, texture and spatial essence as it is about specific ideas; form and content have equal importance. Claire Barclay, for example, often allows the physical properties of her chosen materials to activate her work and guide the form of the finished objects. Combining natural and man-made substances, she says she is drawn to 'hybrid objects that are suggestive of a range of scenarios at once'. A similar sensibility is evident in the work of Ian Kiaer, who arranges his pieces into tableaux reminiscent of theatre sets to evoke particular narratives or ideas. Both these artists select from the low-tech, everyday things around them, manipulating and customising often modest materials. They choose these materials according to their specific aesthetic qualities, finding colour and texture just as important as the objects' inherent references and functional associations. Their objects and images might evoke a narrative or theme by association rather than through literal depiction. Above all there is an ambiguity in their work, an intention to create not one meaning but many. Kiaer and Barclay are not alone in playing with the terms of representation. Their work is deliberately designed to confuse or disrupt a purely intellectual reading, inviting a visceral response. Ultimately the work is about relationships: between the different materials, between the viewer's body and the objects, between the objects and their multiple associations in the world.

Roger Hiorns also works with materials that have a seemingly functional role which he subverts by combining incongruous components such as steel and perfume, or steel and thistles, resulting in a poetic, esoteric aesthetic. Responding to the specific location of the concrete sculpture court at Tate Britain, he introduced a gully – nothing out of the ordinary in itself until it was paired with the symbolic element of fire. By using a material that constantly transforms itself, Hiorns introduced chance or chaos into the work, setting up an intriguing dialogue between the formal and familiar gully and the immaterial flame.

There is an enjoyable tension between the intuitive and the intellectual in the work of Barclay, Hiorns and Kiaer that is also fundamental to David Musgrave's practice. His interest in the representation of the human form is developed through an exhaustive investigation of his chosen media. He manipulates and disguises the inherent properties of traditional materials such as graphite, paint and paper. Created through a process of transference and transformation, his anthropomorphic forms are revealed to the viewer only after a period of concentrated contemplation. It is the cognitive process of gradually recognizing these illusionary figures that ultimately becomes the subject of the work.

Musgrave revels in the enjoyment and skill of making things, in crafting an object and getting to know a material intimately. Claire Barclay's pseudo-functional objects, Muntean/Rosenblum's drawings of disaffected youth and Mark Titchner's hand-carved wooden devotional sculptures all similarly exploit the seemingly outmoded craft aspect of art. Some of the artists who have exhibited as part of the Lightbox programme also celebrate the process of crafting their medium by exploiting the various technologies available. Haluk Akakçe uses computer graphic programmes to create another world for the viewer to escape to – a strange, alternative reality where meanings are never fixed. Katy Dove's animations combine traditional drawing and digital media to create works that are poised between abstraction and figuration, with image and sound delicately balanced to develop or dissolve in tandem.

The body is present in much of the work, though often only by implication. Daria Martin uses the medium of film to explore the movement of the body in space, sharing a fascination with those low-tech, everyday materials espoused by Barclay and Musgrave, which she transforms for her film *Birds* into costumes and props. As in Barclay's sculptural installations, there is a consideration of three-dimensional space that continually shifts as it is navigated. In Barclay's installation we are encouraged to negotiate the space in order to activate the sensory relationship between ourselves and the objects. In Martin's film we take a more passive role as we watch the dancers hold their poses while the amateurishly constructed theatrical set appears to move around them. Simple but precisely performed movements are often at the heart of the videos by John Wood and Paul Harrison too. Using basic props against a minimal backdrop, they test out different actions and their effects, exploring a continuing flux between stasis and movement. In Musgrave's drawings and installations the presence of the figure is implicit, playing on our desire to recognize the human form in what we see. The body recurs more literally in the drawings and paintings of Muntean/Rosenblum, works that are nearly life-size. The most striking aspect of them is the frozen and highly theatrical gestures adopted. Intriguingly, the figures have been choreographed by the artists as much as composed, so that when we enter the exhibition space we also enter a relationship with these characters.

Musgrave's enquiry into the human form is an on-going project that takes on manifest forms, and the same is true for artists such as Ian Kiaer and Mark Titchner. Both appear to be making works that stem from a continuous process of research or investigation, each artist often returning to key sources. The works therefore tend to act as punctuation marks or open-ended propositions, all part of a work-in-progress in which a number of ideas interrelate rather than culminate in a final thesis. The attempt to illustrate particular concepts or give a realistic representation of the facts is resisted. Rather, these works present a highly subjective and fictionalised scenario in which various narratives free-associate according to a deeply personal logic.

Titchner appropriates the ideas put forward by the marginal theorists of a now out-dated avant-garde and interweaves them with texts pulled from other eclectic sources, allowing his works to become a sort of composite experimental mechanism in which different theses collide and often ultimately cancel each other out. Divorced from their original context, his tracts and slogans encourage multiple readings. Similarly, Kiaer unites eccentric, historical visionaries through what he perceives to be their shared aspirations for artistic pursuit or their desire to integrate man and environment. Time and geography are concertinaed to create complex, fragmentary narratives. This subjective ordering of objective information to present new, imaginary propositions allows the works to operate on many levels, and sets up a demanding relationship with the viewer. These works can at first appear inscrutable; the references are not immediately apparent and any clear reading is thus deliberately thwarted. Yet as viewers we 'inhabit' their installations, and we are encouraged to take part in the investigation. If we choose to probe deeper, information reveals itself. Moreover, the works maintain a visual coherence that captures the essence of their subject. Titchner's rudimentary hand-carved sculptures invoke notions of labour and devotion, carrying totemistic references. Likewise, Kiaer eloquently captures the whimsical, fragile nature of his protagonists' lofty ambitions through the ephemeral nature of his objects, simultaneously elevating the humble props while grounding the aspirations they represent.

The notion of the work functioning as an open-ended enquiry rather than presenting a closed proposition defines a tendency common to many of these artists. A narrative is often implied but not fulfilled, threading its way through the work in intriguing ways, whether through Titchner's use of disparate texts, Muntean/Rosenblum's pairing of word and image, or even Mark Lewis's nostalgic tour through a failed modernist housing estate, in which the action takes place in the margins of the frame. The fact that Lucy McKenzie chose to call her filmed performance *Oblique Composition* implies a certain mystery, opening up the work to interpretations that are ultimately inconclusive.

Many of the artists we included delve into history without bearing its burdens too heavily. They re-cycle the past freely, taking the view that cultural heritage is as current and available as everything else. And they demonstrate how art history can be re-used, not just as inspiration or mere quotation but as basic raw material. Thus it is not only theories and ideas that re-surface. Artists like McKenzie re-animate historical forms, borrowing imagery from extant sources, picking through both the mainstream and the marginal, the ideas of recent decades and of centuries past. In her projects to date she has used the ephemera of the Olympic Games, interior design magazines, the Arts and Crafts style of Charles Rennie Mackintosh, to name but a few, and she also maintains a long-standing fascination with an Eastern Bloc aesthetic. Her elegant paintings, prints and murals are infused with past ideas and coloured with a seductively nostalgic sensibility, but they have powerful relevance to the present and to their immediate environment. The same is true of Mark Titchner, who borrows widely, from William Morris's decorative motifs to psychedelic 1970s graphic art. McKenzie and Titchner mix elements of the high street with art history, and Paul Morrison does the same when locating the imagery for his landscape paintings. His recent excursions into film-making further bear this out; the film he showed in the Lightbox programme was an artful elision of footage from disparate sources, drawing from marginal as much as mainstream cinema.

Nigel Cooke is another artist who mixes his sources but makes something from them that is entirely his own. The scale and subject matter of his canvases propose comparisons with landscape painting of the nineteenth century. His sublime heavens and desolate territories have a powerful resonance with the paintings of the Pre-Raphaelites or the American Hudson River School. However, Cooke updates his metaphysical visions with ghoulish imagery plucked from cult horror films – Halloween pumpkins and severed heads rendered in an appropriately overwrought style. The same curious collision of past and present occurs in the paintings of Muntean/Rosenblum. Their protagonists adopt the reflective poses of characters from Christian iconography found in Renaissance panel painting, but such motifs are often obtained secondhand, pillaged from advertisements and fashion photographs in contemporary lifestyle magazines. Rendered as large-format tableaux vivants and paired with text, these works might prompt us to think of the allegories presented in Pre-Raphaelite paintings, but only masquerade as profound statements; in fact they are as intentionally meaningless and empty as the sources from which they are derived.

The critic and curator Nicolas Bourriaud has used the term 'postproduction' to articulate the way in which much of the art made today 'samples' a diversity of forms, styles and cultures, and finds fresh use for them, inserting them in alternative narratives. That he made comparisons to the music industry and DJ-ing seems particularly pertinent when considering the work of artists like Oliver Payne and Nick Relph. They use their films to create an audio-visual collage, and although this technique overlaps with the earlier film-making styles of John Maybury and Derek Jarman, Payne and Relph would claim a wider array of influences, ranging from MTV pop promos and old BBC documentaries to the more recent films of Harmony Korine. Moreover, the pulsating, eclectic visual language they use references almost every aspect of youth culture, street style, and forms of music from punk rock to Country and Western, mounting a visual and aural cacophony.

Art Now aims to reflect themes and concerns in current British practice. However, guided by the enthusiasms of a shifting curatorial team, it does not attempt to be impartial and wholly representative of the many different types of work being made today. Key to the programme's currency is its responsive nature. This publication provides the opportunity to reflect back with the benefit of hindsight on a series that came together and moved on quickly.

Lizzie Carey-Thomas, Mary Horlock and Katharine Stout

List of works

17 May – 6 July 2003

Mark Titchner

BE ANGRY BUT DON'T STOP
BREATHING
2003
Mixed media
Dimensions variable
What makes a man start fires
2003
Hand-carved wood, acrylic paint
100 × 200 × 2 cm
All work courtesy the artist
and Vilma Gold, London

7 June – 31 August 2003

Roger Hiorns

Vauxhall
2003
Steel and fire
Dimensions variable
Courtesy the artist and Corvi-Mora,
London

19 July – 7 September 2003

David Musgrave

Paper golem
2003
Aluminium and acrylic paint
83 × 41.5 × 5.5 cm
Drawing
2003
Graphite on paper
37 × 32 cm
Giant torn tape figure (grey)
2003
Silk emulsion paint
470 × 1332 cm
Painted form no. 2
2003
Epoxy putty and enamel paint
9 × 5 × 1.9 cm
All work courtesy the artist and
greengrassi, London

19 July – 14 September 2003

Lightbox 1

19 – 27 July 2003

Breda Beban

Walk of Three Chairs
2003, 16 mm film, 10 min
Courtesy the artist and
Film and Video Umbrella

28 July – 3 August 2003

Ann Course in collaboration
with Paul Clark

Waiting for Waste
2000, video, 3 min
Recruitment Video
2000, video, 3 min
The Artist
2000, video, 3 min
Mother
2000, video, 1 min
Untitled
1999, video, 1 min
Black Magic
2003, video, 2 min
Shit Belt
2000, video, 3 min
All work courtesy the artists and LUX

4 – 10 August 2003

Mark Lewis

Children's Games (Heygate Estate)
2002, Colour Super-35mm film,
transferred to DVD, 7 min 23 sec
Courtesy the artist and
Film and Video Umbrella.

11 – 17 August 2003

Dan Holdsworth

Anechoic
2003, DVD, 6 min 22 sec
Sound Design: Welburn Kispert
Courtesy the artist

18 – 24 August 2003

Oliver Payne & Nick Relph

Mixtape
2002, video, 23 min
Courtesy Gavin Brown's enterprise,
New York

25 – 31 August 2003

Phil Collins

Baghdad Screentests
2002, DVD, 47 min
Courtesy Kerlin Gallery, Dublin

1 – 7 September 2003

Jaki Irvine

Actress
2003, Super 8 and DVD, transferred
to DVD, 3 min 40 sec
Actress: Ilaria di Luca
Courtesy the artist and
Frith Street Gallery

8 – 14 September 2003

Saskia Olde Wolbers

Placebo
2002, DVD, 6 min
Courtesy the artist and Maureen
Paley/Interim Art, London

20 September – 9 November 2003

Lucy McKenzie

View from Oxford Street,
Glasgow 1980
2003
Charcoal drawing
76 × 56 cm
View to Ballater Street, Glasgow 1980
2003
Lino and silkscreen print
51 × 51 cm
Oblique Composition
2003
(with Paulina Olowska)
DVD, 10 min
MMIV
2003
Colour silkscreen/offset print
59.5 × 84 cm
All work courtesy the artist and
Cabinet, London

22 November 2003 – 25 January 2004

Ian Kiaer

Brueghel project/studio
2003
Fibreglass and aluminium builders
board, cardboard and acetate,
watercolour and acrylic on taffeta
Dimensions variable
Collection of Mariano Pichler, Milan
Courtesy Alison Jacques Gallery,
London
Wittgenstein project/Skjolden
2003
Found plastic waste bin, upturned,
pink styrofoam, plastic fragment,
watercolour and acrylic on rip-free
taffeta
Dimensions variable
Collection of Ann and Marshall Webb,
Toronto
Courtesy of Alison Jacques Gallery,
London
Brueghel project / Casa Malaparte
1999
Acrylic on calico, balsa wood,
cardboard, foam, artificial moss, stool
Dimensions variable
Private collection, London
Courtesy Alison Jacques Gallery,
London

Wittgenstein Project: Palm House
2002
Vinyl on canvas, watercolour on
cardboard, polystyrene, painted
card model stuck on polystyrene,
acetate and cardboard model
Dimensions variable
Collection Wilfried & Yannicke
Cooreman, Puurs (Belgium)
Courtesy Alison Jacques Gallery,
London

22 November 2003 – 15 February 2004
Lightbox 2

22 November – 14 December 2003
Daria Martin
Birds
2001, 16mm film transferred onto DVD,
7 min 30 sec
Courtesy the artist
15 December 2003 – 4 January 2004
Katy Dove
I'm so Ashamed
2001, animation with sound, 1 min
Melodia
2002, animation with sound,
background watercolour by the artist's
grandfather George Wilson, music I
kut by Jorg Maria Zeger, published by
the sampler 'colour and pattern',
apestaartje 2002, 4 min 30 sec
You
2003, animation with sound, 5 min
30 sec, commissioned and produced
for Zenomap for the Venice Biennale
with the support of the Scottish Arts
Council and the British Council
All work courtesy the artist
5 January – 25 January 2004
Haluk Akakçe
Birth of Art
2003, DVD, 4 min
Soundtrack: Michael Vecchio
Courtesy the artist and Cosmic
Galerie, Paris
26 January – 15 February 2004
Rob Kennedy & Stuart McGregor
You're Not Blank
2002, video, music by Un Caddie
Renverse dans L'herbe (remixing
Janek Schaefer), 2 min 20 sec,
commissioned by Shadazz for the
compilation 'Evil Eye is Source'
Courtesy the artists

7 February – 28 March 2004
Nigel Cooke
Silva Morosa
2002 – 2003
Oil on canvas
183 × 244 cm
Sing the Pumpkin Song
2003
Oil on canvas
183 × 274.5 cm
Ghost on the Happy Trails
2003
Oil on canvas
183 × 366 cm
Mirrors
2003
Oil on canvas
183 × 366 cm
All work courtesy the artist and Modern
Art, London and Andrea Rosen Gallery,
New York

17 April – 20 June 2004
Muntean / Rosenblum
Untitled (The Paradox of Our Time...)
2004
Acrylic, pencil and cut-out paper on
canvas
235 × 400 cm
Collection Vanessa Branson, London
Untitled (We Believed, Though...)
2004
Acrylic on canvas
200 × 250 cm
Courtesy Maureen Paley/Interim Art,
London
Untitled (At A Time When...)
2004
Acrylic, pencil and cut-out paper on
canvas
225 × 275 cm
Collection John A Smith and Vicky
Hughes, London
At the Beginning Was...
2004
MDF, aluminium, and paint
400 × 500 × 200 cm
Courtesy Maureen Paley/Interim Art,
London
Various Works on Paper
2004
Dimensions variable
Courtesy Maureen Paley/Interim Art,
London
It Is Never Facts That Tell
2004
DVD, 5 min, 16 mm film transferred
onto DVD
Courtesy Maureen Paley/Interim Art,
London

3 July – 12 September 2004
Claire Barclay
Deadfall 1
2004
Aluminium, hide
100 × 300 × 300 cm
Deadfall 2
2004
Aluminium, leather
400 × 300 × 300 cm
Askance
2004
Aluminium, brush fibre
100 × 200 × 30 cm
Sharp Dusk
2004
Aluminium
7 × 5 × 15 cm
Bird Psyche
2004
Wood, leather, steel wire
150 × 300 × 150 cm
All work courtesy the artist and
doggerfisher, Edinburgh

3 July – 5 September 2004
Lightbox 3

3 July – 25 July 2004
Rosalind Nashashibi
Hreash House
2004, 16 mm film transferred
onto DVD, 21 min 8 sec
Courtesy the artist
26 July – 15 August 2004
Paul Morrison
Satellite
2004, film transferred onto DVD,
3 min 18 sec (on 20 minute loop)
Courtesy the artist and Alison Jacques
Gallery, London
16 August – 5 September 2004
John Wood and Paul Harrison
66.86m
2003, video, 3 min 30 sec
1km
2004, video, 2 min 15 sec
100m
2004, video, 3 min 50 sec
All work courtesy the artists and fa
projects, London
(*1km* funded by Arts Council England,
South West)

Biographies

Mark Titchner
Born in Luton, 1973
1991 – 1992
Hertfordshire College of Art and Design, London
1992 – 1995
Central St Martin's College of Art and Design, London
Lives and works in London
Selected Solo Exhibitions
2003
I We It, Platform for Art, Gloucester Road Tube Station
We Were Thinking of Evolving, Vilma Gold, London
Do not attempt to reform man, We are what We are,
Galerie Jorg Hasenbach, Antwerp
2001
Love, Work & Knowledge, Vilma Gold, London
1999
Vilma Gold, London
1998
One in the Other, London
Selected Group Exhibitions
2004
Sodium and Asphalt, A British Council Touring Exhibition,
Museo Tamayo Arte Contemporaneo, Mexico City touring
to Museo de Arte Contemporaneo de Monterrey
2003
Electric Earth, A British Council Touring Exhibition
2002
The Galleries Show, Royal Academy of Arts, London
2001
Playing amongst the ruins, Royal College of Art, London
City Racing (A Partial History), ICA, London
1999
Heart & Soul, 60 Long Lane, London
1998
Surfacing, ICA, London
1996
LIFE / LIVE, Museé d'Art Moderne de la Ville de Paris

Roger Hiorns
Born in Birmingham, 1975
1991 – 1993
Bourneville College of Art, Birmingham
1993 – 1996
Goldsmiths College, London
Lives and works in London
Selected Solo exhibitions
2003
UCLA Hammer, Los Angeles
Corvi-Mora, London
Marc Foxx, Los Angeles
2001
Corvi-Mora, London
Selected Group exhibitions
2004
A Secret History of Clay, Tate Liverpool
Particle Theory, Wexner Center for the Arts, Ohio
2003 / 2004
Still Life, A British Council Touring exhibition: Museo de
Bella Artes, Caracas; Museo de Arte Carrillo Gil, Mexico
City; Biblioteca Luis Angel Arango, Bogota; Museo de Arte
Contemporaneo, Panama; MAC, Rio de Janeiro; SESI,
Sao Paulo
2002
Exchange, Richard Salmon Gallery, London
The Galleries Show, Royal Academy of Arts, London
2001
Looking With / Out, East Wing Collection,
Courtauld Institute of Art, London
2000
... comes the spirit, Jerwood Gallery, London
Shot in the Head, Lisson Gallery, London
1999
Heart and Soul, 60 Long Lane, London
1998
True Science, Gallery K, Hamburg
1997
European Couples and Others, Transmission Gallery, Glasgow

David Musgrave
Born in Stockton-on-Tees, 1973
1992 – 1993
Wimbledon School of Art
1994 – 1997
Chelsea School of Art
Lives and works in London
Selected Solo exhibitions
2004
greengrassi, London
2002
Transmission, Glasgow
2001
greengrassi, London
2000
greengrassi, London
1998
Duncan Cargill Gallery, London
Selected Group exhibitions
2003
Anna Barribal and David Musgrave, Arnolfini, Bristol
David Musgrave and Roger Hiorns, Mark Foxx, Los Angeles
2002
Shimmering Substances, Arnolfini, Bristol; Cornerhouse,
Manchester
2001
Casino 2001, S.M.A.K, Ghent
2000
British Art Show 5, toured nationally to Edinburgh,
Southampton, Cardiff, Birmingham
1999
Limit Less, Galerie Krinzinger, Vienna
Heart and Soul, 60 Long Lane, London
Manufacturers, Paper Bag Factory, London
1997
Transmat, One in the Other, Tenter Ground, London
1996
Banana Republic, Covent Garden, London

Lightbox 1

Breda Beban
Born in Novi Sad, Yugoslavia, 1952
Selected Solo Exhibitions
2003 – 2004
I Can't Make You Love Me, Southampton City Art Gallery;
Newlyn Art Gallery, Penzance.
Ann Course and Paul Clark
Both born in 1965
Live and work in London.
Selected Group Exhibitions
2004
East End Academy, Whitechapel Art Gallery, London
2003/2004
A Century of Artists Film in Britain, Tate Britain
2003
Other Than Film, Rotterdam Film Festival, Rotterdam
Mark Lewis
Born in Hamilton, Canada, 1965
Lives and works in London
Selected Group Exhibitions
2003
Rooseum, Malmo, Sweden
2002
Liverpool Biennial, Liverpool
Dan Holdsworth
Born in Welwyn Garden City, 1974
Lives and works in London
Selected Solo Exhibitions
2003
The New Art Gallery, Walsall
Selected Group Exhibitions
2003
Centre for Contemporary Photography, Chicago
Oliver Payne and Nick Relph
Oliver Payne
Born in London, 1977
Nick Relph
Born in London, 1979
Live and work in London and New York
Selected Solo Exhibitions
2001
The Essential Selection, Gavin Brown's enterprise,
New York
Selected Group Exhibitions
2003
Beck's Futures 4, ICA London
Days Like These, Tate Triennial, Tate Britain
Utopia Stations, 50th Venice Biennale (Golden Lion award)

Phil Collins
Born in Runcorn, Cheshire, 1970
Lives and works in Brighton
Selected Solo Exhibitions
2004
Ormeau Baths Gallery, Belfast
Selected Group Exhibitions
2003
Witness, Barbican Art Gallery, London
Brighton Biennial

Jaki Irvine
Born in Dublin, 1966
Lives and works in Dublin
Selected Solo Exhibitions
2004
Solo Screening, Kerlin Gallery, Dublin
2002
Holding it all together, Gallerio Massimo Re Carlo, Milan

Saskia Olde Wolbers
Born in Breda, The Netherlands, 1971
Lives and works in London
Selected Solo Exhibitions
2004
Maureen Paley/Interim Art, London
2003
Statement, Diana Stigter Gallery, Art Basel
2002
Burro Friedrich, Berlin

Lucy McKenzie
Born in Glasgow, 1977
1995 – 1999
Duncan of Jordanstone College of Art, Dundee
(BA Hons Fine Art)
1998
Erasmus Exchange to Karlsruhe Kunst Akademie, Germany
Selected Solo Exhibitions
2004
Bi-Curious, Cabinet, London
Deathwatch, Van Abbemuseum, Eindhoven
2003
Nova Popularna, Foundation Galerie Foksal, Warsaw
(with Paulina Olowska)
Brian Eno, NAK Aachen, Germany
2002
If It Moves, Kiss It, Galerie Christain Nagel, Berlin
2001
Global Joy, Galerie Daniel Buchholz, Köln
Heavy Duty, Inverleith House, Royal Botanic Gardens,
Edinburgh (with Paulina Olowska)
2000
Decemberism, Cabinet Gallery, London
Selected Group Exhibitions
2003
Venice Bienniale
2002
Painting on the Move, Kunsthalle Basel, Switzerland
The Best Book About Pessimism I Ever Read,
Kunstverein Braunschweig, Germany
2001
Here and Now: Scottish Art 1990 – 2001,
DCA / various venues, Dundee / Aberdeen
Circles, ZKM, Karlsruhe
Painting on the Edge of the World, Walker Art Center,
Minneapolis
2000
Dream of a Provincial Girl, M3, Sopot, Gdansk, Poland
Beck's: Futures, ICA, London, Cornerhouse, Manchester,
CCA, Glasgow
2000
British Art Show 5, Edinburgh, Southampton, Cardiff,
Birmingham
*It May Be a Year of Thirteen Moons, But it's Still the Year
of Culture*, Transmission Gallery, Glasgow

Ian Kiaer
Born in London, 1971
1991 – 1995
Slade School of Art, University College London
1998 – 2000
Royal College of Art, London
Lives and works in London
Selected Solo Exhibitions
2004
Galleria Massimo de Carlo, Milan
2003
Endless Theatre Project, Tanya Bonakdar Gallery, New York
Ian Kiaer / Jeff Ono, aspreyjacques, London
Interstice / Double Impact, W139, Amsterdam
2001
aspreyjacques, London
Selected Group Exhibitions
2004
Wider than the Sky, 117 Commercial Street, London
Empty Garden-2, Watari-un, Watari Museum of Contemporary Art, Tokyo
2003
Happiness, Mori Art Museum, Tokyo
Delays and Revolutions, Biennale di Venezia, Venice
2002
Building Stuctures, P.S.1 Contemporary Art Center, New York
Artists Imagine Architecture, ICA, Boston
2000
UBS Painting Prize, Whitechapel Art Gallery, London
Manifesta 3, Ljubljana
1999
New Contemporaries 99, Sir John Moore's, Liverpool; Beaconsfield, London

Lightbox 2

Daria Martin
Born in San Francisco, 1973
Lives and works in London
Selected Solo Exhibitions
2003
Analix Forever Gallery, Geneva
2001
Andrea Rosen Gallery, New York
Selected Group Exhibitions
2004
In the Palace at 4am, Alison Jacques Gallery, London
2003
The Moderns, Museo Castello di Rivoli, Turin
Katy Dove
Born in Oxford, 1970
Lives and works in Glasgow
Selected Group Exhibitions
2004
A Kind of Bliss, The Drawing Room, London;
Mead Gallery, University of Warwick
2003
Frieze Art Fair Film and Video Programme, London
Zenomap, Scottish Pavilion, 50th Venice Biennale
Prague Biennale
Haluk Akakçe
Born in Turkey, 1970
Lives and works in London
Selected Solo Exhibitions
2004
The approach, London
Museum für Gegenwartskunst, Basle
2003
The Drawing Room, London
Selected Group Exhibitions
2004
Beck's Futures 5, ICA, London
Rob Kennedy and Stuart McGregor
Rob Kennedy
Born in London, 1968
Lives and works in Glasgow
Selected Group Exhibitions
2003
Zenomap, Scottish Pavilion, 50th Venice Biennale
Stuart McGregor
Born in Glasgow, 1970
Lives and works in Glasgow

Nigel Cooke
Born in Manchester, 1973
1999 – 2004
PHD in Fine Art, Goldsmiths College, London
1995 – 1997
MA Painting, Royal College of Art, London
1991 – 1994
BA (Hons) Fine Art, Nottingham Trent University
Lives and works in London
Selected Solo Exhibitions
2004
Andrea Rosen Gallery, New York
2002
Modern Art, London
2000
Nigel Cooke, CHAPMAN Fine ARTS, London
Selected Group Exhibitions
2004
Sodium and Asphalt, A British Council Touring Exhibition,
Museo Tamayo Arte Contemporaneo, Mexico City touring
to Museo de Arte Contemporaneo de Monterrey
Monument to Now, Dakis Joannou Collection Foundation,
Athens
Edge of Real, Whitechapel Art Gallery, London
2003
Group Exhibition, Gallery Sommer, Tel Aviv
Works on Paper, Jack Hanley Gallery, San Francisco
I See A Darkness, Blum & Poe, Los Angeles
Dirty Pictures, The approach, London
Exploring Landscape: Eight Views From Britain,
Andrea Rosen Gallery, New York
2002
Still Life, A British Council Touring Exhibition, travelling
to Museo de Bellas Artes, Santiago; Museo de
Bellas Artes, Caracas; Museo de Arte Carrillo
Gil, Mexico City; Biblioteca Luis Angel Arango, Bogota;
Museo de Arte Contemporaneo, Panama City; Museo de
Arte Moderno, Guatemala; MAC Nieroi, Rio de Janeiro;
SESI, Sao Paulo
Melodrama, ARTIUM, Centro-Museo Vasco de Arte
Contemporaneo, Vitoria-Gasteiz, Spain, travelling
to Centro José Guerrero, Palacio de los Condes
de Gabia, Granada
2001
Tattoo Show, Modern Art, London
1998
New Contemporaries 98, Tea Factory, Liverpool, travelling to
Camden Arts Centre, London;
Hatton Gallery, Newcastle
1997
Interesting Painting, City Racing, London

Muntean/Rosenblum
Markus Muntean
Born in Graz, Austria, 1962
Adi Rosenblum
Born in Haifa, Israel, 1962
Muntean/Rosenblum have worked in collaboration since
1992. They live and work in London and Vienna
Selected Solo exhibitions
2004
Austrian Centre for Contemporary Art, Melbourne
2003
Maureen Paley/Interim Art, London
There is A Silence to Fill, Salzburger Kunstverein, Salzburg
2002
To Die For, De Appel, Amsterdam
Billboards, Kunsthaus Bregenz
2001
Lost in the savage wilderness of civil life,
Georg Kargl, Vienna
Summer Contemporary, Tel Aviv
2000
Where else, Secession, Vienna
I always tell you the truth unless of course I am lying to you,
Kunsthaus Glarus
1999
Franco Noero, Torino
Selected Group exhibitions
2004
26. Biennale Sao Paulo, Sao Paulo
Seven Sins, MUSEION, Museum fur Moderne
und Zeitgenössische Kunst, Bozen
2003
Taktiken des Ego, Lehmbruck Museum, Duisberg
Rituale, Academie der Künste, Berlin
2002
Contemporary Art Projects, Seattle Art Museum, Seattle
The Galleries Show, Royal Academy of Arts, London
2001
The City of tomorrow and the exhibition year One, Bo01,
Malmo
Berlin Biennale, Berlin
2000
Fantasies and Curiosities, The Art Museum, Miami
1999
Blue Fire, International Biennial of Young Art, Prague
1998
The Campaign Against Living Miserably, Royal College
of Art, London
Lifestyle, Kunsthaus Bregenz

Claire Barclay
Born in Paisley, Scotland, 1968
1986 – 1990
Glasgow School of Art
1991 – 1993
Glasgow School of Art
Lives and works in Glasgow
Selected Solo Exhibitions
2003
Ideal Pursuits, Dundee Contemporary Arts
2002
Some reddish work done at night, doggerfisher, Edinburgh
2000
Homemaking, Project Space, Moderna Museet, Stockholm
Take to the Ground, The Showroom, London
1997
Out of the Woods, Centre for Contemporary Art, Glasgow
Selected Group Exhibitions
2003
Zenomap, Scottish Pavilion, 50th Venice Biennale
2002
Howl, Canberra Contemporary Art Space, Australia
Early One Morning, Whitechapel Art Gallery, London
2001
Here and Now, Dundee Contemporary Arts
2000
If I Ruled the World, Part 2, Centre for Contemporary Arts, Glasgow
Bush Mechanics, Catalyst Arts, Belfast
Museum Magogo, Independent Studios, Glasgow and Stripp Gallery, Melbourne
1999
If I Ruled the World, The Living Art Museum, Reykjavik
1998
Nerve, Glasgow Projects, Artspace, Sydney
Clean and Sane, Edsvik Konst Och Kultur, Stockholm and Gallery f15, Moss, Norway

Lightbox 3

Rosalind Nashashibi
Born in Croydon, 1973
Lives and works in Glasgow
Selected Solo Exhibitions
2004
CCA Glasgow
Kunsthalle Basel
2003
Visions For the Future V, Fruitmarket Gallery, Edinburgh
Selected Group Exhibitions
2003
Zenomap, Scottish Pavilion, 50th Venice Biennale
Beck's Futures 4, ICA, London
Midwest and Midwest Field, CCA Cinema, Glasgow
Displaced, Hammer Projects, UCLA Hammer Museum, Los Angeles
Some Things We Like, aspreyjacques, London

Paul Morrison
Born in Liverpool, 1966
Lives and works in London
Selected Solo Exhibitions
2004
Cheim and Read, New York
2003
Saxifraga, Galleria d'Arte Moderna e Contemporanea, Bergamo
Haematoxylon, Irish Museum of Modern Art, Dublin
Mesophylle, Magasin, Grenoble
Selected Group Exhibitions
2004
Art of the Garden, Tate Britain
Rose C'est La Vie, Tel Aviv Museum, Israel
2003
Flower Power, Musée des Beaux Arts, Lille

John Wood and Paul Harrison
John Wood
Born in Hong Kong, 1969
Lives and works in Bristol
Paul Harrison
Born in Wolverhampton, 1966
Lives and works in London and Bristol
Selected Solo Exhibitions
2003
Hundredweight, fa Projects, London
2002
Twenty Six (Drawing and Falling Things), Chisenhale Gallery, London; touring to Northern Gallery for Contemporary Art, Sunderland
Selected Group Exhibitions
2004
Density+/-0, Ecole Nationale Superieure des Beaux-Arts, Paris
2003
MIT List Visual Arts Center, Massachusetts
A Century of Artists Film in Britain, Tate Britain
2003/2004
Still Life, A British Council touring exhibition,

Acknowledgements
The curators would like to thank all the artists who have participated in Art Now, their galleries, and all the lenders to the exhibitions.

Photographic credits
Front cover image: Rodney Tidnam and Dave Lambert
Mark Titchner: Mark Heathcote and Caroline Shuttle
David Musgrave: Mark Heathcote
Roger Hiorns: Rodney Tidnam and Dave Lambert
Lucy McKenzie; Mark Heathcote and Caroline Shuttle
Nigel Cooke: Mark Heathcote and Caroline Shuttle
Muntean/Rosenblum: Caroline Shuttle
Installation view of Gloucester Road: Steve White
Claire Barclay: Caroline Shuttle
Mark Heathcote (details)
Breda Beban: Film and Video Umbrella

All other images are courtesy the artists and their galleries.